P9-ELI-230

Creating and Maintaining Organized Files and Records

Written by Marla Benson
Edited by National Press Publications

NATIONAL PRESS PUBLICATIONS

A Division of Rockhurst College Continuing Education Center, Inc.
6901 West 63rd Street • P.O. Box 2949 • Shawnee Mission, Kansas 66201-1349
1-800-258-7248 • 1-913-432-7755

National Press Publications endorses nonsexist language. In an effort to make this handbook clear, consistent and easy to read, we have used "he" throughout the odd-numbered chapters, and "she" throughout the even-numbered chapters. The copy is not intended to be sexist.

Creating and Maintaining Organized Files and Records

Published by National Press Publications, Inc.
Copyright 1998 National Press Publications, Inc.
A Division of Rockhurst College Continuing Education Center, Inc.

Printed in the United States of America

1 2 3 4 5 6 7 8 9 10

ISBN 1-55852-230-1

Table of Contents

INTRODUCTION

Do you feel "organizationally impaired"? Do you want to scream as more and more paper lands on your desk? Do co-workers or family members comment about the piles of paper on your desk...credenza...chairs...floor...? Do you have stacks of paper on everything? Do you have trouble deciding where a paper or a computer file should go? How the file cabinet should be organized? What the folder headings should say so you can actually find them again?

Information overload is a very real issue today; and it gets worse with each new phase of technology. Paper and computer files, e-mail, voice mail and the Internet...decisions, decisions, decisions. Where will I put it? How long should I keep it? And most importantly, how will I find it again?

During moments of disorganization (when it takes more than 60 seconds to find what you need), how do you feel? Frustrated, incompetent, embarrassed and stressed?

During moments of organization, on the other hand, when you can immediately locate what you need, don't you feel confident, relaxed, powerful and in control? What a difference!

Organization is great but it is *not* the goal; *all its positive by-products are what we really want.* By reducing stress, increasing confidence and creating an aura of competence, organization helps us reach our fullest potential, think more clearly and make better decisions.

Even the most organizationally impaired can conquer the mess that lurks in the file cabinet, computer system, on the desk and surrounding areas. It simply requires an assessment of why you want to be organized and a decision about how important it is to you.

What You Will Learn from This Handbook

For many people filing is the last item on their list of priorities. If they can find what they need...even if it's at the last minute...that's good enough.

Filing is generally not held in high regard. It's considered a boring, tedious, unimportant "no-brainer." While it may not be as exciting as many other tasks, the importance of good record keeping cannot be denied.

Record keeping is the lifeblood of any organization. Without records, there is no history, nothing to base future business decisions on. Without records, there is no record of employee accomplishments, no way to track the contributions you make in your working life. Without records, there is no way to show how money flows out or flows in to see "how we're doing."

In this handbook you will learn, step-by-step methods for creating a filing system that works. One that is simple, efficient, smooth, easy to use and that grows with you and your changing needs. Specifically, you will learn:

- The solid organizational concepts that will carry over to your home and other areas of your life, including better organized workspace, personal records, closets, cabinets, drawers, and storage areas.

- How to slot the time required to create the new system, train others in the office to understand it and how to gain their cooperation for its continued efficiency.

- What supplies you need, where to find them and how to stay up-to-date on the newest organizing tools and products.

- How to create a disaster recovery program to prepare your office and home for real-life emergencies such as fires, floods, earthquakes and other disasters.

- Super Tips that make the process even quicker and more fun.

Whatever your organizational issues and problems, the principles, techniques, tips and exercises in this book will help you gain...and keep...control.

1 REALITY CHECK

Everyone knows someone who seems naturally organized. But nobody is born with an organizational gene. Organization is a learned skill like driving a car. There are just as many reasons people aren't better organizers as there are different kinds of information to organize.

1. People were never taught how to organize. Many people think each kind of data has its own special, very complicated method of organization. Not true. The basic concepts, principles and techniques easily apply to organizing all of the following kinds of information:

- Current paper (paper you are using)

- Filed paper

- Computer files — on a hard drive or LAN (Local Area Network)

- E-mail

- Voice mail

2. Too many product choices. With so many organizing tools, it's hard to know which are the right ones for the job. What kind of file cabinets, hanging folders, internal folders, color-coding tools or other items would assist in creating the best possible system?

3. Everyone in the office files differently! Having one set of rules is critical for those sharing files in a central filing system. Everyone "doing his or her own thing" doesn't work. A set of guidelines or procedures resolves these concerns.

4. "In the past I always had an assistant to do the organizing." Many people today find themselves with expanded areas of responsibilities, including the creation and maintenance of filing systems. The existing system needs to be understood so routine filing can be done; inadequate filing systems need to be restructured to enhance efficiency and productivity.

5. Not sure why the current system doesn't work. Assessing the current system is key to the success of designing a new system or improving an old one. Questions must be answered about access, logistics, and many other issues including:

- How to find the time to reorganize the system

- How to keep the new system going and updated

- Where to obtain industry-specific information regarding retention schedules and disaster recovery plans

- How to control the avalanche of paper coming your way

- Creating the paperless office

The Organizational Survey: Identifying Trouble Spots

Assessing current strengths and weaknesses is the first step in moving toward an optimal organizational system. Complete the following survey, answering each question with a yes or no.

Organizational Survey

	YES	NO

Paper Filing
1. Does each person in the office have his or her own filing system?
2. Are people always coming to you asking where they can find something?
3. Do people refer to the same item with different terms, making it difficult to decide where an item should go? (For example, "dog," may also be referred to as "canine," "hound," or "puppy.")
4. Are the file cabinets too full?
5. Do you have trouble locating files only to find they are on other people's desks?
6. Are the same documents filed in more than one place?
7. Do you regularly have trouble gathering the necessary documents for meetings?

Office Space
8. Do you have trouble deciding where a certain piece of paper should go?
9. Are items that demand your attention today mixed in with other items?
10. Is your "To Be Filed" bin further away than arm's reach?
11. Do you keep papers "just because"?
12. Would it take several hours to get through your "To Be Read" pile?
13. Have you ever gone into the office during off-hours to get back filing done?
14. Does your inbox act as a storage place?

High Tech Items (Personal Computers, E-mail, Voice Mail)
15. Do you create clever ways to identify computer files, but still have trouble finding them later?
16. Is most of your incoming e-mail in the same folder?
17. Are routine distribution items, such as memos, sent out on paper even though e-mail is available?
18. Do you spend more time than you think you should trying to find a specific computer file?
19. Are you uncomfortable creating folders or directories/subdirectories with your computer software? (MAC or Windows)
20. Do you keep e-mail or voice mail "just because"?

If you answered yes to five questions or more, the skills you will learn in **Creating and Maintaining Organized Files and Records** will serve you well. If you answered yes to 10 questions or more, read faster.

Chapter 1 Summary

Organization is a learned skill, not a genetic gift. There are numerous reasons people aren't better organizers.

1. People were never taught to organize.

2. Too many product choices available.

3. Everyone does it differently!

4. "I always had an assistant to do the organizing."

5. Not sure why the current system doesn't work.

An Organizational Survey will help you assess strengths and weaknesses relating to paper filing, office space and high-tech items (computers, e-mail, and voice mail).

2 WHAT YOU GOTTA KNOW BEFORE YOU REORGANIZE ANYTHING

The five key considerations that constitute the foundation for any filing system include what you need to know about organizing paper/computer/e-mail files and why a good system is necessary.

Key Consideration #1:
Keeping Paper Costs a Lot of Money

The paper in your office is getting out of control and you are running out of places to put it. Before thinking about what to keep, where to put it and how to get your hands on it, you need to focus on its cost.   Consider these facts:

- Eighty percent of everything we file is never used again.

- The typical office generates twice as much paper as needed (thanks to the copier and computer printer).

- In the average organization, 75 cents of every dollar can be spent on record keeping. Consider the following costs:

    a) purchasing/leasing file cabinets

    b) supply costs — folders, paper, labels, etc.

    c) square footage costs — additional space required for cabinets (rent plus insurance, heating/cooling)

- Fully 75 percent of file cabinet space is wasted or inappropriately used:

  a) Twenty-five percent of file cabinet drawers contains inactive or archive records that should be stored elsewhere at lower cost.

  b) Fifty percent of the space is either empty or contains supplies.

  c) Only 25 percent of a typical file cabinet contains active files that are actually used.

Key Consideration #2:
Making an Honest Assessment of Your Current System

Take a hard look at your current filing system. Be as honest and objective as you can in answering the following questions:

1. Does it work? Can I quickly find what I'm looking for? Is it logical?

2. Do I like it? Is it physically convenient? Do the headings on folders, etc. make sense?

3. Where do I spend my time? Are you in the office most of the time? Are you an "on the go, on the run" kind of person who conducts business from the car or at other facilities? Your storage decisions will differ depending on your responses.

4. Does it work for others? If you are sharing information and files with other people, ask questions 1, 2 and 3 on their behalf.

Key Consideration #3:
Giving Your Cabinets an Identity

Every place in the office has to have a clear identification: every file cabinet, blueprint cabinet, drawing cabinet, even bookcases and disk/tape storage. Each needs to be identified by a name or number, for example, "This is Cabinet 1 (Bertha); counting from the top, this is Drawer 1, Drawer 2, Drawer 3, Drawer 4." The next cabinet over is Cabinet 2 (George); again the drawers are counted from the top, #1, #2, #3, #4.

Bertha   **George**

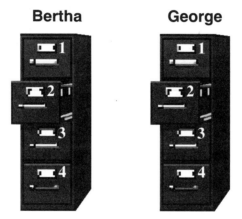

This kind of specific numbering is much better than the common response you get when asking where something is: "No, no, not that cabinet, the next one over — no, no, not that drawer; the second from the bottom, not the top!!" Exasperating, isn't it? The beauty of numbering/naming the cabinets is that you can simply state, "That will be found in Cabinet 2, Drawer 3," or "That will be found in George, Drawer 3."

SUPER TIP!

Abbreviate when indicating a location in writing; for example, Cabinet 2, Drawer 3 would be identified as C2D3 or George 3.

Key Consideration #4:
Eliminate Overcrowded File Cabinets by Adopting the Document Life Cycle

The Document Life Cycle is designed to help you make the most of the space you already have by separating the items you are likely to use (active storage), from the items you are unlikely to use, but need to have access to (inactive storage) from the items you keep primarily for legal or tax purposes but will probably never touch (archive).

Here's how you will use the Document Life Cycle:

1. You create or receive a document.

2. You use it.

3. You ask yourself if you need to keep it or not.

   If the answer is no, you toss or recycle.

   If the answer is yes, you decide among the following three options:

a. Items you are likely to use — active storage — cabinets closest to you.

b. Items not likely used but that need to be accessible — inactive storage — elsewhere in the building.

   Review inactive folders every two years. Ask yourself, "Has this folder been used in the last four years?" If the answer is yes — leave it in inactive storage. If no, ask "Do I need to keep it?" If the answer is no, you toss or recycle it. If the answer is yes, you move the folder to archive storage.

c. Items kept primarily for legal and tax purposes, and not likely to be used — archive storage — boxed in a lower cost location such as a warehouse.

Keeping the Document Life Cycle Plan Alive

Active Files

- **Review active files annually.** The first time you go through the active file cabinets, you MUST review every document in every folder. Ask yourself if this folder has been used in the last two years. If yes, retain in active files. If no, ask "Might I need it this next year?" If yes, move to inactive files. If no, "Do I need to keep it?" If yes, move to archives. If no, discard or recycle.

- **Make an appointment on your calendar for your annual active file review.** Choose a time of year when you are least likely to be interrupted and most likely to stick to your schedule. Estimate the time required and block it off as a priority item.

SUPER TIP!

Use color-coded year labels to speed up the process of separating active folders from inactive folders. Place a color-coded year label on each folder as it is created. For example, if the folder is created in 1998, place a 1998 label on it. If the same folder is then used the next year (meaning "referred to" or "added to"), place a 1999 label over the 1998 label. This shows that it was active in 1999.

Inactive Files

- **Review inactive files every two years.** Ask yourself, "Has this folder been used in the last four years?" If yes, leave in inactive; otherwise ask "Do I need to keep it?" If yes, move it to archive storage. If no, discard or recycle.

- **Make an appointment to review inactive files following your active file review.** Estimate the time required and block it off as a priority item.

Archive Storage

- **Archive storage review is guided by your records retention schedule** (detailed in Chapter 6).

- **Pack folders to be archived in letter- or legal-sized storage boxes** available from office supply stores and catalogs in varying grades of cardboard and plastic.

- **Create an inventory list on your computer** of the contents of each box. This list should contain the folder's names and the retention destroy date if you know it.

SUPER TIP!

Print out two copies of the inventory list.

Place one on top of the contents of the box before putting on the lid.

Place the other one in a plastic sheet protector and tape it to the front of the box. It is common for boxes to be stacked on top of one another in storage. If the list is taped to the front, it's less likely to be obscured and you can see what the content is without having to open the box.

- **Number each box.** Be sure that your numbering system does not duplicate that of another department within your organization.

- **Write the box number on all sides of the box** using a black marker. When marked like this, no matter where the box is placed, the box number will show clearly.

SUPER TIP!

To find an archived folder quickly, be sure the box number is included on your computerized inventory list. Open the inventory document on your computer and use the Find feature to locate the number of the box in which the folder will be found.

- **Pack cardboard storage boxes tightly in case of fire.** Fire departments indicate that even if there is a fire at the archive location, many times records in tightly packed cardboard boxes survive. Think about it — no oxygen to fuel the fire!

SUPER TIP!

Put the retention destroy date both on the box and in the inventory list. When it is legally all right to destroy records, make sure you do so. Records that are kept past the legal destroy date can be subpoenaed and used against you in a court of law. Make it as easy as possible to keep up with these dates by marking them properly.

SUPER TIP!

Many organizations are moving away from keeping paper versions of archive documents by using Document Imaging. The documents are scanned using a high level scanner and a computer with Optical Character Recognition (OCR) software, which attempts to recognize each character from the original document. The archives are then stored onto CD-ROM or microfilm. Often times, the original hard copies of the documents do not need to be kept, the scanned version becomes the legal archive. Check with your legal counsel for specific guidance.

Key Consideration #5:
"Usage Determines Storage": Three Words of Wisdom

Think of these three words when making just about every organizing decision: The way you use things determines where you put them. By keeping these words in mind, you will make better decisions.

That is exactly what you have done with your active, inactive, and archive files. You want the folders that are used the most close at hand — active. The folders that you may need but haven't used in two years are placed elsewhere in the building — inactive. Finally, the folders that you have to keep for legal or tax purposes but haven't actually used in four years or more can be placed in another building — archived.

EXERCISE: "Usage Determines Storage"

The following is a list of the items in your medicine cabinet. The items you use most are placed on Shelf 1, the shelf that is the easiest to reach. Items you use occasionally go on Shelf 2 and items you use rarely go on Shelf 3. Place the shelf number you would select next to the following items:

Item	Shelf #
Headache medicine	
Bandages	
Rubbing alcohol	
Razor/shaving cream	
Thermometer	
Dental floss	
Contact lens products	
Toothpaste	
Cough medicine	
Cotton balls	

Reflections

Can you imagine someone telling you there was a right or wrong way to store your medicine cabinet items? That's crazy! There is no right or wrong sequence because you put things away according to the way you use them. People who wear daily contact lenses might keep contact lens products on Shelf 1, but people who wear disposable lenses might keep contact lens products on the top shelf because they are rarely used.

This same philosophy is true in designing your filing systems, directories/subdirectories, and e-mail folders. There is no right or wrong system. You customize according to the three words of wisdom, "Usage Determines Storage."

Chapter 2 Summary

1. Keeping paper costs a lot of money.

   Remember, the more paper you keep, the more it costs your organization. Keeping the paper is worth the cost only if the paper is actually used. Statistics show, however, that most of what we keep is never used.

2. Make an honest assessment of your current filing system.

   - Analyze each organizational issue — filing cabinets, computer files and workspace — with these questions.

     — "Is it working?"

     — "Do I like it?"

     — "Does it work for others?"

3. Give your cabinets an identity.

   For ease of directing others to a particular location each place in the office is to be named or numbered. For example Bertha, Drawer 1; Cabinet 1, Drawer 2; and so on.

4. Eliminate overcrowded file cabinets by adopting the Document Life Cycle.

   Separate the files in the file cabinet into the following categories:

   — Active files (ones you actually use)

   — Inactive files (those you may use, but have not used in two years)

   — Archive files (those that have not been used in four years or more, but are kept primarily for legal or tax purposes)

5. "Usage Determines Storage": Three Words of Wisdom

   Continually ask yourself how you use items to determine where they should be stored. Items most used are kept closest to you; the lesser-used items are kept further away.

3 DESIGNING A PLACE FOR EVERYTHING: PART 1

Everyone has heard the saying: A place for everything and everything in its place! As of right now, it's not likely that you even know what you have, much less if it is in the right place. Now that you have the foundational principles from Chapter 2, you need to take Steps 1 and 2 of the Seven Step Process required to create the best possible filing system.

Step 1:   Make a List of What You Currently Have

Step 2:   Get a Handle on the Rules of Alphabetizing — It's Not Just "A through Z" Anymore

Step 1. Make a List of What You Currently Have

You must know what you have before you can appropriately determine what you need. Remember the statistic: 80 percent of everything filed is never used again. Reviewing the contents of the cabinets is not enough; everything needs to be listed into a document on your computer. This list will serve you well as you reorganize and maintain your system.

- It begins as the list of current folders, allowing for thorough review and planning.

- It is then rearranged into the proposed categories/subdirectories.

- In its final form it will act as the index. The index is used to help maintain the system over time, allowing you to determine the exact location of any folder, active, inactive, or archive, as well as retention destroy dates if known.

What does this list look like? What headings will it have?

- **All folder headings:** Whatever the label on the folder says is what gets typed into the list.

- **Keywords** (optional)**:** If the folder headings are not descriptive enough, select and type in other words that pertain to this folder — other ways you might identify it. These are called keywords.

- **Folder locations:** Use the cabinet identification number described in Chapter 2. For example, C1D1 is Cabinet 1, Drawer 1.

- **Status:** Whether the folder is active, inactive, or archived. Abbreviate as follows:

  A = Active, I = Inactive, AR = Archive

- **Retention destroy date** (if you know it)

What software do I use to make this list?

Choose the type of software with which you have the greatest comfort level and which offers the greatest flexibility. Here are some options in order of preference.

1. **A database program** will give you the most flexibility for manipulating the list over time. For example, you will be able to sort the list alphabetically, numerically or by date. You can query (ask it certain questions) and the program gives you the extract answers in a separate list. Questions might include "List all folders that have a retention destroy date in the year 1998," or "List all folders containing BUDGET- 1997." Popular database programs include: Microsoft Access™, Lotus' Approach™ and Corel's Paradox™.

2. **A spreadsheet program** would be your next choice if you were already comfortable with one. Most spreadsheet programs include database capabilities so you will be able to sort, query and extract. Popular spreadsheet programs include Microsoft Excel™ and Lotus 1-2-3™.

3. **A word processing program** with a table format might be your third choice. The table format will give you much more flexibility than just typing a list. You will be able to change the table with cut and paste, and sort. Popular word processing programs include Microsoft Word™ and Corel's WordPerfect™.

Widget Co.				
Folder Name	**Keywords (optional)**	**Location**	**Active Inactive Archive**	**Retention Destroy Date**
Holiday Party — Catering		C4D4	A	
Holiday Party 1997 — Guest List		C4D4	A	
Insurance — Auto 1995		C12D2	I	
Photographs — Catalog 1994			AR Box 17	2000
Photograph — Catalog 1998		C4D2	A	
Receipts — Office Supply		C1D3	A	
Receipts — Postage		C1D3	A	

SUPER TIP!

Use a handheld tape recorder to make this job easier. Rather than standing in front of all the cabinets with a yellow pad and pen, get a handheld recorder and speak into the internal microphone. Start by identifying where you are, "I'm at Cabinet 1, Drawer 1"; then read off all the folder names. Do the same with each cabinet and later transcribe the tape into the program you've selected on your computer.

Handheld recorders can be found at most stores that sell small electronics. Desirable features include:

— Variable playback speeds — play the tape back at a slower than recorded speed for easier transcription.

— Uses regular-size cassette tapes so you can listen to tapes as well as record.

— Headphones for portability.

SUPER TIP!

Keep the recorder with you in the car to record your ideas and to-dos as they flash through your mind.

Step 2. Get a Handle on the Rules of Alphabetizing — It's Not Just "A through Z" Anymore

To develop an efficient alphabetic system, it's helpful to know the "Rules of the Road." An agreed upon set of alphabetizing rules is important not just for your use, but for others who will be using the system as well. Everyone needs to know these rules to avoid misfiling, a system breakdown and files disappearing into a black hole.

The rules shared here are the rules of alphabetizing for a traditional paper filing system, and they still hold true today. The ability to sort or alphabetize on a computer is slightly different, however, as computers sort everything into strict alphabetical order. You may want to bend the traditional rules a bit, encouraging greater compatibility between the paper and computer files.

- **Strict alphabetical order:** Smith, James comes before Smith, Joan. File by last name first. For last names that are the same, alphabetize by the first name until there is a difference between the two.

- **Mc:** Many people like to have a separate filing section for names beginning with Mc, such as McDonald. This is perfectly acceptable; however, the more modern method is to file such words in strict alphabetical order because this is how the computer will sort these items. If alphabetized by computer software, this is how these same files would be organized.

MacDonald	filed as MAC
McDonald	filed as MCD
McHenry	filed as MCH

- **Numbers:** Arabic and Roman numerals are filed in numeric order before the alphabetical filing; therefore, numbers are filed together in their own section, usually in Cabinet 1, Drawer 1, because they come before A-Z.

  — 1-Hour Photo Developing

  — 5-Minute Car Wash

  — 30-Minute Lube & Oil

- **Symbols:** More and more companies are using symbols as the first character of their names. This can cause a lot of confusion for those who don't know the rules.

  — Symbols, like numbers, are filed in their own section prior to the alphabetical filing, usually in Cabinet 1, Drawer 1.

  — Spell out (in your head) what the symbols represent, then file alphabetically.

     # becomes the word "number"

     $ becomes the word "dollar"

     & becomes the word "and"

     So, these three symbols would be filed in the following order: &, $, #

- **Rule 1 for the word "the"— leave it out.** In traditional paper filing systems, the words "the," "of," "and," "at," and other throwaway words are left out leaving only the key words as part of the folder heading or label.

  Example:

  The Medical Center at the University of Southern California becomes:

  Medical Center — University Southern California

- **Rule 2 for the word "the"— place it at the end.** If the word "the" is the first word, and is part of the official name, put it at the end, leaving the key words as the first ones you will see on a label.

  The Book Place becomes   *Book Place, The*

  The Time Tunnel Video becomes   *Time Tunnel Video, The*

- **Punctuation.** Words with punctuation are filed in alphabetical order, leaving out the punctuation symbol. This is also how your computer will sort.

  O'Connor   filed as *OC*

  O'Leary   filed as *OL*

- **Hyphenated words.** Hyphenated names can cause a great deal of confusion when filing. Consider them as one word and file by the first letter of the first part of the name.

  For example,

  Martha Brown-Smith   filed under B, for Brown

  This same name without a hyphen is filed as follows:

  Martha Brown Smith   filed under S for Smith

- **Company names that are a person's name.** Such names are filed by the first letter of the first word in the organization's name when filing alphabetically.

  Joe Smith Plumbing   filed under J for Joe

  Joe Smith Publishing   filed under J for Joe

  Because there is more than one Joe Smith, carry the alphabetizing out until there is a difference between entries. In this case, Plumbing would come before Publishing.

Chapter 3 Summary

1. Make a list of what you currently have.

    Use a handheld tape recorder to read off and then transcribe what folders you currently have and where they are. Use the suggested computer format so the list will only need to be typed in once. It can then be modified as needed to create a file system index. The index will help you find any folder in less than 60 seconds.

2. Get a handle on the rules of alphabetizing — It's not just "A through Z" anymore.

    A blend of traditional and computer alphabetizing rules is recommended. Understanding these will help you to decide if alphabetical is the best system for your needs. Rules of alphabetizing also need to be clearly understood by everyone using the filing system.

4 DESIGNING A PLACE FOR EVERYTHING: PART 2

Now that you have made a list of what you have (Step 1) and gotten a handle on the rules of alphabetizing (Step 2), it's time to tackle Steps 3 and 4 of the Seven Step Process to create the best possible filing system.

Step 3: Create Clear, Simple Categories/Subcategories and Directories/Subdirectories

Step 4: Streamline by Cross-Referencing

Step 3. Create Clear, Simple Categories/Subcategories and Directories/Subdirectories

Deciding on major groupings, categories/subcategories and directories/subdirectories* is the most important determination to be made about your organizational system. Is it best filed alphabetically? By subject? Numerically? This area of designing your system takes a great deal of thought and customization.

*Categories/subcategories are how you refer to the major groupings for paper files. Directories/subdirectories are how you refer to the major groupings for your computer files. The same questions, concepts and principles apply to both paper and computer. For ease of reading in this section, both categories/subcategories and directories/subdirectories will be referred to as categories and subcategories. Chances are your current filing systems are in either alphabetical or subject order; most people are stuck in the alphabetical or subject filing rut. Nothing is wrong with these systems; but they are not your only choices.

No one knows how your files are used better than you do. No one can tell you what will be the best system for you, just as no one can tell you the best way to organize your medicine cabinet. Here are some guidelines and questions to consider, however, to help you create the simplest and most logical system for you and your needs.

Create Clear, Simple And Logical Categories Using SPACNG

Use this acronym to help you remember your choices:

S ubject

P riority

A lphabetical

C hronological

N umerical

G eographical

Subject Filing

Two important things you need to know about subject filing: (1) it is the most commonly used filing system and (2) it can be the least accurate filing system because items are filed from one's own viewpoint. Each person may think of the same item differently, using different terminology. So when one person looks for something, it may be by a different subject heading than when somebody else looks for it. Needless to say, confusion, frustration and wasted time often result.

Examples:

- "Staff" could also be referred to as "personnel," "employees," "crew," "faculty," or "cast."

- "Rules" could also be referred to as "guidelines," "procedures," "policies," "regulations" or "codes."

- "Publications" could also be referred to as "periodicals," "magazines," "journal," or "circular."

When Should You Use Subject Filing?

Subject filing is best used when:

1. Category headings are well known by everybody who is using the system.

2. The title of the category begins with a noun. For example, major headings might be "Clients," "Personnel," or "Suppliers." These headings will later be broken down further into subcategories.

Priority Filing

As the name implies, priority filing is used to organize items in order of importance. This system is often used for projects that involve many different tasks which are then organized in order of importance — starting with the tasks that are most important to those that are least important.

Alphabetical Filing

This system is easy for others in the office to learn and use. Just make sure that they understand the rules of alphabetizing to keep files out of the black hole. It is an excellent choice if you are clear about what you are looking for. For example, in alphabetical filing, client names would be mixed in with all other alphabetical items such as vendors, suppliers etc. If you know the client name, it will be easy to locate. If you don't know the client name, you will have great difficulty locating the file when mixed with other types of files.

Chronological Filing

Chronological filing sorts items in order of date. Chronological files are commonly used for payroll files, project files, and correspondence files.

Chronological filing is used when you want to show:

- history — the date order in which items occurred

- future — the date order in which items will occur

Numerical Filing

Numerical filing is the most accurate filing system because items are filed sequentially by number: 1, 2, 3, 4, 5 etc. It is best used for items that already have a number assigned, such as purchase orders (by the P.O. number) or payroll (by the check number or personnel number).

SUPER TIP!

Don't assign numbers to items strictly for filing purposes. This is not how you will think about these items when looking for them. If you were to use such a system, you would constantly be searching the index to look up what number was assigned to the item you are looking for making you less efficient.

Remember: "Usage Determines Storage."

Geographical Filing

As implied by its name, geographical filing is done by a place or location. For example, it could be according to state, city, zip code, zone, or region.

Now that you have reviewed the most common filing options, let's put your new-found knowledge to the test! Explore the different ways you could organize the following list of movies using SPACNG as your guide. Think carefully about each option of SPACNG. Your first conclusion is not the only one and may not be the best for your needs.

- Field of Dreams

- Rocky

- It's a Wonderful Life

- The Wizard of Oz

- E.T.

- Jurassic Park

Reflections

Subject Filing

- type of movie: Is it classic, adventure, romance, comedy, or children's?

Priority Filing

Priority filing may de done in order of importance or, in this case, your preference. Start with the one you like best to the one you like least or vice versa.

Alphabetical Filing

- by film title

- by director's name (Capra, Spielberg, etc.)

- by star's name (Costner, Garland, Stallone, Stewart, etc.)

Chronological Filing

- by date the movie was filmed or released

- by the date you viewed it last

Numerical Filing

- by stock or item number

Geographical Filing

- by story location (Iowa, Kansas, Philadelphia, etc.)

- by filming location

Do this same SPACNG exercise with the following items. Try to get as many category types to fit as you can. Be outrageous. Don't look for the one and only perfect choice, but explore what is possible.

Personnel files:

Breeds of dogs:

Insurance files:

Authors:

Two Questions to Help You Decide on the Best Categories

Now that your mind is opened to various possibilities, how do you decide which is the best choice? Remember "Usage Determines Storage," and ask yourself these questions.

- How do I (we) use the files? Do we use them by subject? By name? How?

- How do others ask for the files? If they come to me (us) for assistance in finding files, how do they ask? Are they asking by a client name? By subject? By when the documents in the file are due?

Selecting the Most Appropriate Top Level Category/Directory

This chart is a guide to selecting the most appropriate category; but just like organizing a medicine cabinet, you will need to decide which is most appropriate for your needs.

	Y/N	Subj.	Prior.	Alpha.	Chron.	Num.	Geo.
1. Are there 20 files or fewer?	Y	📁	📁				
2. Is this a sole-user system?	Y	📁	📁				
3. Are there more than five people using the system?	Y			📁		📁	
4. Are there more than 10,000 files?	Y			📁		📁	
5. Are geographic subdivisions appropriate?	Y						📁
6. Is it important that the system be highly accurate?	Y			📁		📁	

Subcategories/Subdirectories

Once you have determined your top-level, broad categories, use SPACNG again to determine appropriate subcategories.

Example: For personnel files, maybe you selected geographical as a top-level category. Perhaps you have different offices and choose to separate personnel by office. While geographical filing is a great start, it is not enough. You will also need to determine subcategories. Perhaps the next level would be numeric, by employee number or social security number; or alphabetical, by employee name. The next level may be benefit items per employee, etc.

Texas Division

      Barker, Jan

          401(k)

          Health Insurance

          Stock Options

      Jones, Chris

          401(k)

          Health Insurance

          Stock Options

      Silver, Pat

          401(k)

          Health Insurance

          Stock Options

The same questions you asked when deciding on categories are also asked when deciding on subcategories:

- How do I (we) use the files? Do we use them by subject? By name? How?

- How do others ask for the files? If they come to me (us) for assistance in finding files, how do they ask? Are they asking by a client name? By subject? By when the documents in the file are due?

Subcategories should be logical, working from the broad top-levels that you have decided. Limit the number of subcategory levels to no more than five or six levels. Additional levels make it more difficult. Once you create too many subcategories, you will have to depend on your memory to find them rather than being able to locate them logically.

SUPER TIP!

These same concepts apply to your computer directories and subdirectories. If you are not comfortable with creating and maintaining directories, subdirectories, copying, moving, and deleting of files, make a point of learning this utility on your computer. In Windows 3.1, the utility is called the File Manager, in Windows 95™ it's called Explorer and for a Macintosh system use folders.

EXERCISE

Divide the following supermarket list into categories, subcategories and items. Some items in the list are department headings; some are sub-headings, and some you will find within a department. The rules of this exercise are:

- Find the top-level categories first, then work your way down to subcategories and department items.
- Use each item only once.
- Don't add any new items. Everything you need is in the list.
- Remember the three words of wisdom: "Usage Determines Storage."

Administrative	Dishes-R-Clean Detergent
Advertisements	Fitzgerald, Ivy
Avery, Susan	Gingerbread Yummies
Benefits	Jones, Harvey
Beverages	KCBS
Bubble's Cola	Lots-O-Crunch Potato Chips
Buttermilk	Lowfat Milk
Buyers	Perfectly Clear Soda
Casper's Cottage Cheese	Radio
Check-Out Personnel	Snack Items
Cookies	Snap-E-Pop Popcorn
Coupon Catalogs	Staff
Dairy	Sudso Laundry Detergent
Dashing, Don	Television
Detergent	Vendors
	Yolo's Yogurt

Reflections

If you were to distribute this list to multiple people, it's likely that each person would come up with a slightly different result. Some areas may not be completely clear or may even cross over one another. For example, KCBS may be both radio and television. Ivy Fitzgerald may be part of administrative but also be a buyer. When items could be placed in more than one subcategory, cross-referencing is often a solution.

EXERCISE

Apply this new-found knowledge of categories and subdirectories to your filing system. Access the computer list of folders that you created in step one of this chapter. Cut and paste it into the list of proposed categories, subcategories, and files beneath each. Do not physically move the files yet. You're working on the computer list only at this time so you can alter and review the plan before physically reorganizing the files.

EXERCISE

Brainstorm on how the questions that helped you decide on categories and subcategories for the filing system can also be used to organize the following:

- e-mail into folders

- Internet bookmarks, otherwise known as Favorite Places

Reflections

Step 4. Streamline By Cross-Referencing

Streamline by cross-referencing when it would be perfectly logical to file the same item in more than one place. Cross-referencing can eliminate confusion and wasted space.

Using a cross-referencing system helps you decide where an item should be filed. This minimizes indecision and the resultant stacks and piles of items on your desk that you just aren't sure what to do with. It also, by default, alleviates the frustration and confusion that goes along with the indecision and mess. No longer do you have to be concerned that as soon as you choose a place to file it, someone will ask for it using different terminology and you won't be able to find it.

In the Organizational Survey how did you answer the following questions? If any of your answers were yes, cross-referencing will be a valuable tool for you.

- Do people refer to the same item with different terms, making it difficult to decide where an item should go? (For example, "dog," may also be referred to as "canine," "hound," or "puppy.")

- Are the file cabinets too full?

- Are the same documents filed in more than one place?

- Do you have trouble deciding where a certain piece of paper should go?

Cross-Referencing Systems

There are two kinds of cross-referencing; simple cross-referencing and the cross-reference sheet.

Simple Cross-Referencing

Filing a confusing name. If you needed to make a decision about filing the name Ying Monito Bo, what would you decide? Should it be filed by Ying? or Bo? or even Monito? When unsure of a surname, file it by the last word in the sequence. Then place a cross-reference in the other place that it is likely for people to look. Ying Monito Bo; file it under Bo, the last word in the sequence. Under Ying, you will place a cross-reference place holder labeled "Ying Monito Bo, see Bo." Simple cross-referencing to the rescue.

When a person changes his/her name: Here is a common scenario when people are tempted not to use cross-referencing. Example: You have a personnel file for a co-worker named Mary Jones. You have worked with Mary for many years and always think of her as Mary Jones. But, Mary Jones is changing her name to Mary Smith. Because you work with her and know her, even after the name change, you have left her file as Mary Jones. You get a new employee into the office that sees filing to be done for Mary Smith and creates the Smith file. Now the new employee is filing under Smith, but you continue to file under Jones. You have just created a perfect example of the black hole. What should be in one file is now in two pieces.

Here's how simple cross-referencing solves this problem. As soon as Mary Jones changes her name to Mary Smith, we create a new Smith folder. We then take her old folder and convert it into the placeholder by placing a label on it that indicates "Jones, Mary see SMITH, MARY." Now anyone looking under Jones will be referred to the correct filing place, Smith.

When a company changes its name: This is the Mary Jones scenario once again. When a company we have known for years changes its name, we are often tempted to leave the folder in the old location. Make the change and leave the cross-reference placeholder.

When a person or company has a formal name and a commonly used alias: An example being the need to create a folder for J.C. Penney. Do we file this in alphabetical order under J for the first letter of the company name? Or do we file it under its commonly known name of Penneys? The decision is yours according to the earlier topic "Usage Determines Storage." Ask yourself "How do I (we) use it?" and "How do people ask for it?"

What's important is that you make a decision then create a simple cross-reference placeholder in the other location where people are likely to look for it.

```
SUPER TIP!

Use these suggestions for simple cross-referencing
placeholders.

• A cardboard divider with a tab on top for the label.

• Use the backflap of a standard manilla folder (with the
  tabs on it). Cut off the front of the folder so it cannot
  mistakenly be used as a file folder.

• Color-code the label on the placeholder. Use a color
  of label that you don't use for anything else in the
  office. For example, hot orange. When you see the
  hot orange color, it will signal to your brain that the
  item is a cross-reference, not a file folder.
```

Cross-Reference Sheet

A cross-reference sheet is used when the same document has multiple topics and could be placed in more than one existing folder. Here's a scenario to illustrate why and how it works.

You work in the personnel department of the organization. A memo has been circulated regarding changes in benefit policies; retirement, sick leave and vacation pay. Because you are in personnel, you already have separate folders for each of these three topics. Do you photocopy and file this three times? You could, but a better solution is to make a decision about the most likely place that this will be used, let's say vacation pay, then place cross-reference sheets in the other two folders (Sick Leave and Retirement).

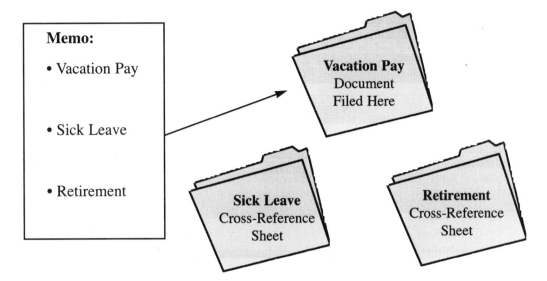

Here's how you will create and use the cross-reference sheets:

- The cross-reference sheet is stapled to the inside cover of the existing folder(s) (in this case retirement and sick leave).

- Create the cross-reference sheet in a word processor, preferably in a table format. Headings are Document Name/Number, Date and Located. Be sure to extend the table so that the rows fill the page.

- You will use the same form in the folder over and over until all lines are filled.

Cross-Reference		
Document Name/Number	Date	Located

Each time you have a document that could be filed in this folder, but have chosen to file it elsewhere, fill in the form by hand. Indicate the name or number of the document that could be filed here, the date of the document that could be filed here and where you chose to file it.

SUPER TIP!

Color-code the cross-reference sheet paper in a color that you don't use for anything else. Then coordinate the paper color with the color of label used for cross-reference placeholders. For example, if you use hot orange for the cross-reference placeholder label, also use hot orange for the cross-reference sheets.

Do not use cross-referencing for a folder that must be complete at all times. For example in a legal environment, client files must be complete at all times. It would not be appropriate to cross-reference items from the client file, have an attorney take the client file to court only to find that items are missing because they were cross-referenced.

Chapter 4 Summary

1. Create clear, simple categories/subcategories and directories/subdirectories.

   The biggest decisions you will make about reorganizing the filing system are choosing categories and subcategories. To help you decide, always remember "Usage Determines Storage" and ask the two questions:

   — "How do I (we) use the files?"
   — "How do people ask for the files?"

2. Streamline by cross-referencing.

   Cross-referencing saves space, time, money and confusion. Use the two cross-referencing techniques to cut back on duplicate filing.

   — Simple cross-referencing (placeholders in file drawers)
   — Cross-reference sheet (inside existing folders)

5 BRINGING YOUR SYSTEM TO LIFE

Now that you have made the most crucial, critical decision regarding the filing system, it's time to prepare for the physical reorganization by completing Steps 5, 6, and 7.

Step 5:   Use Color-Coding to Save Time and Money

Step 6:   Choose the Best Office Supplies for Your Filing System

Step 7:   Get Everything in Its Place: Physically Reorganize the Files

Step 5.   Use Color-Coding to Save Time and Money

Color-coding is the easiest tool to increase efficiency in filing and in retrieving files. Studies show that on average, up to five percent of all records are misfiled. The estimated cost of a lost business record is over $100, so using color-coding to minimize lost files can dramatically reduce costs. Studies have shown that color-coding also saves between 30 and 50 percent of filing time.

The purpose of color-coding is to answer questions about the location, content or purpose of an item without having to actually read or open it. The colors do the work by visually sending a message to the brain about the item. (Remember the "hot orange" cross-reference example in Chapter 5. When your eye sees hot orange, whether on a label or a sheet of paper, your brain immediately registers that this signifies a cross-reference.) The color does the work for you.

Tips to consider before creating a color-coding system are:

- Color-coding will be in accordance with the categories and subcategories you have selected.

- Remember the three words of wisdom: "Usage Determines Storage" in designing color-coding systems.

- Choose colors that already signal something in the brain. For example, a high priority folder in red, indicating it is for hot issues, or a budget folder label in green representing money. Using colors that are easily understood will enhance the success of the color-coding system by shortening the amount of time it takes for each person to understand and learn it.

- When appropriate, use all tools in the same color to represent the same thing. For example, blue labels, blue binders, and blue folders are all places for benefit information. (Blue signals benefits to the brain.)

- Color-coding isn't limited to just folder colors and label colors. The same ideas can be used with other supplies like color-coded dots, tabs, sticky notes, binders. Diskette labels, the diskettes and diskette holders, etc.

Color-Coding Ideas Using SPACNG:

Subject	Personnel in yellow, accounting in green, marketing in dark blue
Priority	Today's to-do items in red, tomorrow's items in pink
Alphabetical	A's in red, Bs in light orange, Cs in dark orange
Chronological	First-quarter reports in yellow, second-quarter reports in orange
Numerical	Preprinted numeric labels use a color legend for each number. For example, 0 is pink, 1 is red, 2 is light orange, etc.

Geographical   California in green, Texas in red

Let's explore some other practical ways that color-coding can be adapted.

Idea 1:

Select a different color for each top-level category within the filing system and use that color for both internal hanging folders and corresponding file folders.

Scenario: You are creating a filing system for a city office for each area of responsibility: landscaping, irrigation, road repair, etc.

Solution: Select a different color for each item handled by the city; green for landscaping, blue for irrigation and gray for road repair. A green landscape file folder will only be placed in a green internal hanging folder. A blue irrigation file folder will only be placed in a blue internal hanging folder. A gray road repair file folder will only be placed in a gray internal hanging folder. This makes filing faster, greatly reduces misfiles and helps to identify a file folder when out of the file cabinet. A green file folder on top of a desk tells you that it is a landscape folder. You don't have to read the label to know.

Idea 2:

Select a color of file folder and a different color for its label creating a powerful color-coding combination.

Scenario: You manage all personnel, benefits, and retirement fund files for employees of seven different company divisions.

Solution: Use a different color of file folder for each of the seven divisions: Western division in a yellow file folder, Southern division in a green file folder, Eastern division in a red file folder, etc. Then use a different color label for the types of documents inside, a pink label for personnel, a blue label for benefits and a purple label for retirement.

So, when you see a yellow file folder with a purple label, you know this is a retirement folder for the Western division. When you see a blue folder with a red label, you know this is a benefits folder for the Eastern division. The colors tell you what division the folder is for and what kind of documents are inside without your ever having to open the folder.

Idea 3:

Use color and positioning of the plastic tabs on internal hanging folders to indicate ownership.

Scenario: You are responsible for combining the company President, Senior Vice President and Controller's files into one central system. Since each of them accesses the filing cabinet from time-to-time, you want to design the system so that they can easily retrieve their own items without looking through each other's materials.

Solution: Consolidate the files into an alphabetical system. Then assign a different color and position of internal hanging folder plastic tab for each person. For example, red tabs positioned on the right side of the drawer indicates the President's materials, yellow tabs in the center position of the drawer indicates the Senior Vice President's materials, and green tabs in the left position of the drawer indicates the Controller's materials.

Color-Coding Labels for Open Filing Systems

Labels have been specially designed for open filing system folders. Color-coded alpha and numeric labels are particularly beneficial allowing you to see the name or number on a label without actually having to read it. The label has the letter or number imprinted on it in the assigned color.

Here is an example of a standard way of using color-coded alpha labels for an open filing system. A folder for Jan Moody has three labels on the lower portion of the tab, one for each of the first three letters in the last name, M, O, O. This assists in filing because all Ms are together and are the same color, let's say light green. Then all of the MOs are together. That would be light green for M, then blue for O. Then all of the MOOs are together. That would be light green for M, then blue for O, then another blue for the next O. Another standard white label is also placed on the label tab with the full last and first name of the person. The color-coded labels get us in the right section of the filing system in the cabinet and then we do the remainder of the filing according to the rest of the name on the standard label.

SUPER TIP!

Be sure to use the same brand of labels each time you purchase color-coded alpha or numeric labels. Each brand has their own color-coding legend. For example, not every vendor uses light green for M, and blue for O, so you can see where mixing brands could cause major problems.

Step 6. Choose the Best Office Supplies For Your Filing System

These days it's no longer just four-drawer cabinets, green hanging files and manila folders. The office supply industry is an ever-changing one with new innovations in materials and technology affording more choices than ever. The decisions you make in choosing supplies are important; these items will live with you and your filing system for a long time. The more folders you have, the more expense involved, so you want to educate yourself fully before proceeding.

Filing Cabinets

This is one investment you only want to make once, so purchase the best quality cabinet that you can afford. In addition to the standard four-drawer vertical filing cabinet, look at other types of cabinets: lateral, rotary, five-drawer and open shelving. These have been designed to house more folders in less space. For example, a rotary file can hold the same number of records as three four-drawer cabinets while using as little as one-fourth the floor space.

Considerations before shopping and buying file cabinets:

- How much floor space do you have for active files once the inactive and archive files are housed elsewhere?

- Will the cabinets be in an individual's office space or in a central area?

- Are locking cabinets required for housing confidential files?

- What are the budget considerations?

- Do you need to purchase all new cabinets or do you want to add to what you currently have?

Folders

Folders are divided into two categories, internal hanging folders that go into the file cabinet and file folders that are placed inside the hanging folders.

Internal Hanging Folders

Internal hanging folders, commonly referred to as Pendaflex™ folders, are to be placed inside a file cabinet drawer. The purpose for the internal hanging folder is to indicate where a particular folder should be placed within the filing system. Open file cabinets do not use or require the internal hanging folders.

Internal hanging folder considerations:

- Some people like to use internal hanging folders without file folders. While this does save space in the cabinets, misfiling is often the result. There is nothing in the file cabinet to indicate where the folder should be placed.

- Both letter- and legal-size internal hanging folders are available. Which do you need?

- Internal hanging folders come in different colors which can be matched to your categories and subcategories, making filing faster and lessening the chances of misfiling.

- The insertable tabs that identify each internal hanging folder come in colors, further enhancing a color-coding system.

- An internal plastic pocket is a feature of many internal hanging folders, providing a place for diskettes, business cards, photographs and other items of irregular shape and size. Would this be useful to you?

- For large volumes of material per internal hanging folder, consider either box-bottom hanging folders, which expand up to 2" capacity, or hanging file pockets, which expand up to 3 1/2".

File Folders

File folders are commonly referred to as manila folders. These are placed inside the internal hanging folder and are used to contain the documents of the folder. When removing a folder from the cabinet, you take the file folder out leaving the internal hanging folder. When you need to replace the file folder, the internal hanging folder shows you where it should go cutting back on misfiles.

File folder considerations:

- For open filing cabinets, you will need end-tab file folders which has a tab for the label on the side of the folder. In the open file cabinet, this label tab is always visible. Standard cabinet drawers require file folders with a tab for the label on the top.

- Both letter- and legal-size file folders are available. Which do you need?

- File folder tabs come in different lengths to accommodate labels. Straight cut folders have no tab, 1/5, 1/2, and 1/3-cut are also available. Review each to determine which length will be best suited to your label needs.

- File folders are offered in different colors, which can be matched to your categories and subcategories and internal hanging folders, making filing faster and lessening the chances of misfiling.

- File jackets are just like file folders but are closed on the sides. This feature is beneficial for filing items of irregular sizes so that they don't fall out of the sides of the folder.

Folder Labels

Many different folder labels are available to assist in not only identifying the contents of the folder, but with color-coding to make filing faster and to make misfiling more difficult.

- Standard file labels come in white and in many colors for color-coding systems.

- Some labels are designed for the personal computer using pre-set templates found in most popular word processing programs.

- File labels designed specifically for the personal computer are further designed for use with specific kinds of printers, such as Laser or Inkjet printers. Be sure to purchase the correct labels for your type of printer.

- Both permanent and removable labels are available. Select the one that is most suited to your needs.

- Handwritten labels are sometimes acceptable. If you choose to handwrite labels, be sure to use a permanent black fine felt-tipped marker and write in all capital letters for the best legibility.

SUPER TIP!

If you create new folders frequently, consider a label machine. Label machines are a convenient way to create legible, color-coded labels one at a time. Standard features include LCD display for reviewing the label before printing, multiple type styles and sizes, underlining and optional tape colors.

Resources

Office supply stores are a great place to start. Review the items displayed and inquire about special orders. Many office supply stores have access to much more than what is displayed on the floor. Once you've made all the initial purchasing decisions, office supply catalogs are a convenient way to reorder.

Surf the Internet to find suppliers and information. Even though a vendor may not be in your geographic region, the Web site can be a wealth of information. Search the World Wide Web using the keywords: filing cabinet, file folders, office supplies, and office products. Many office supply stores also have Web sites so you can review products and place orders on-line.

Industry trade magazines are great places to locate vendors specializing in office supplies for specific industries.

Step 7. Get Everything In Its Place: Physically Reorganize the Files

All the big planning decisions have been made and supplies have been purchased. Now it's time to roll up your sleeves and physically reorganize the files. Realize that the more folders you have the bigger this job will be, so take it one step at a time.

1. Review the list of files that you created in Chapter 4, Exercise 2. Cut and paste this list on the computer until you get it exactly the way you want the files to be arranged (categories, subcategories, etc.). Review again and share this computerized version before digging in. In its final form, this list will be your index.

2. Make appointments with yourself to get the job done. Be sure the other people in your office are aware of the tasks required to complete this filing system goal and enlist their assistance in helping you to schedule the time. TIP: If time allotments are in short bursts, work with one file drawer at a time.

3. Use the Document Life Cycle as described in Chapter 3 to separate the active, inactive and archive files and weed out and destroy items or files that are no longer needed. Once the inactive and

archives are separated, there will be a lot more room for the most important, active files. While going through the files, use the Super Tip of placing color-coded year labels on file folders to indicate if they were active this year.

4. Create and place the new labels for internal hanging folders and file folders. Use nouns to describe the contents. The proper format is: FINANCIAL- Express, Inc. 1999. For folders that are too full, divide the contents into two folders using either of the following two methods.

   • Use Roman numerals: FINANCIAL - Express, Inc. 1999, I FINANCIAL - Express, Inc. 1999, II.

   • Divide chronologically: FINANCIAL - Express, Inc. Jan - June 1999, FINANCIAL - Express, Inc. July - Dec 1999.

5. Place the tabs for internal hanging folders on the front of the hanging folder. The advantage is that when you see that tab, your finger can go right to it, opening just the folder you want.

6. Remove paper clips. If necessary use staples.

7. Remove envelopes from file folders if the return address is available on the filed document.

8. When adding new items to a folder, place the newest items on top/front. This way, when opening a folder, the items used last will be most readily available.

9. Separate confidential files and place them in an appropriate locking cabinet, office or desk.

10. Celebrate your commitment to your commitment—and a job well done!

Chapter 5 Summary

1. Use color-coding to save time and money.

   Select the color-coding tools that are best suited to your file cabinet type and categories and subcategories. Remember that the key to color-coding is for the colors to answer questions about the contents of a file folder, diskette, etc. without need of opening or even touching the item. The color tells the story.

2. Choose the best office supplies for your filing system.

   Familiarize yourself not just with the basic tools such as internal hanging folders and file folders, but new items as well. The office supply industry continues to offer new tools that could be the perfect solution to your filing and organizing issues. Survey the office supply stores and the Internet to see if the solutions already exist.

3. Get everything in its place: Physically reorganize the files.

   Time to get going on the physical reorganization.

   - Check your index to be sure it's what you want.

   - Make appointments with yourself to get the job done.

   - Do it!

   - Celebrate!

6 MAINTAINING THE FILING SYSTEM

After all of the assessment, planning and reorganizing of the filing system, you want to ensure that the system is understood and continues to function well. To maintain the filing system:

1. Create and Maintain an Index

2. Set Guidelines

3. Keep Track of Files with a Check-Out System

4. Create a Disaster Recovery Plan

5. Establish a Records Retention Schedule

Create and Maintain an Index

An index is a list of all of the folders in the filing system and their locations. Created on the computer and used to track the physical folders in the file cabinet, the index will assist you in finding any folder (active, inactive or archived) in 60 seconds or less. The more people using the file system and the more cabinets and folders involved, the more essential it is that an index be created and used. If the filing system has one user and one filing cabinet, an index is generally not necessary; your categories and subcategories will be sufficient for finding a file quickly.

The list of existing files you created in Chapter 3, then rearranged into proposed categories and subcategories in Chapter 4 is the foundation for the index.

Updating the list after the physical reorganization of the files is the final step in creating the index. If you did not create the list as previously indicated, return to page 18 to create the current files list; then go to page 37 to modify it into proposed categories, etc.

Set Guidelines

Written procedures for how the filing system works are essential for shared filing systems. All details are written out as a word processing document to:

1. **Train new people**. When a new person is going to use the filing system give them a copy of the written guidelines. This saves a tremendous amount of training time and gives them a ready reference for whenever questions arise.

2. **Clear up any areas of controversy**. Those who share a filing system may not always agree on the proper way to do things. Setting the guidelines creates the rules that everyone must abide by to ensure the filing system is used and maintained correctly.

   For example, most users will place new items in the front of a folder so that most recently used items will be in the front when the folder is opened (and this is the recommended procedure). Others, however, prefer to file with the newest items in the back of the folder instead. No problem for sole user filing systems; but with a shared system, it is inappropriate to have each person using a different method. Clearly set guidelines for any and all rules that you want followed.

Here is an example of what guidelines look like and may consist of.

WidgetCo Inc. Guidelines

1. Financials (invoices, payment statements, receivables) filed chronologically — Cabinet 1

2. Clients filed alphabetically — Cabinet 2

3. Color-coding

Clients	aqua folders
Invoices	green folders
Payments	blue folders
Cross-referencing	hot orange folders/labels

4. Rules of alphabetizing

   Hyphenated words are considered one word (Martha Brown-Smith filed under B for Brown)

   Mc - (such as McDonald's) file in alphabetical order. Mc's mixed in with other Ms.

5. Filing chronologically within a folder. Most recently used material in the front.

6. Cabinets are numbered left to right; 1, 2, 3, 4, 5. Drawers counted from the top; Drawer 1, Drawer 2, Drawer 3, etc. The first cabinet, third drawer is referred to as C1D3.

7. The Finance Department uses the "F" drive on the Local Area Network (LAN). Subdirectories are as follows...

The decisions and rules in the guidelines are up to you. The communication, understanding and cooperation of the guidelines are the most important keys to the continuing success of the filing system.

Keep Track of Files with a Check-Out System

Do people in your office take a file out of the cabinet, take it to their offices — never to be seen again? You go to the cabinet and discover the file is missing, without a trace. Then you spend an enormous amount of time trying to locate the file, going from office to office, desk to desk. Unfortunately this scenario is very common in many organizations. Fortunately either one of two simple methods can be used to regain control and keep track of files:

- The out log

- The check-out card system

The out log. A central logbook or clipboard that is signed when a file is removed. It will tell you who has what file at any time. Out logs are easiest to use and enforce when the organization has a file room as opposed to file cabinets out in the open. A file room manager will also help to enforce the out log.

The check-out card system. Can work well in a less structured situation where file cabinets are out in the open and many people have access to them. If it is inconvenient for people to go to a central book or clipboard when signing out files, set up a check-out card system instead. A check-out card is to be signed and placed in the file cabinet in the precise location where the file was housed. This way when you go to the cabinet to locate a file, the card will tell you who has it and when it was removed from the cabinet.

To set up the check-out card system, go to the office supply store to see prefabricated check out cards. They are generally 8-1/2" x 11", come in different colors and sometimes have a pocket. Headings are as follows:

File Name/Number	Taken By	Date

Keep an ample supply of check-out cards and pens available at every file cabinet. People can very quickly fill out the card and then place it on the location where the file was taken.

SUPER TIP!

On storage of check-out cards:

- Place check out cards in an organizer on top of each cabinet.

- Place a supply of check out cards inside the front of each file drawer.

In a perfect world, check-out cards work well; but in the real world people sometimes will not want to bother to fill out the card or use them. "But I only need the file for a minute!" and other excuses abound. If check-out cards are to be successful, they must be enforced — *without exception*. Everyone must use the check-out cards at all times or the system breaks down.

SUPER TIP!

To enforce check-out cards:

- Color-code the check-out cards. If a limited number of people have access to the filing system, assign a different color check-out card to each person. That way, people do not have to fill out the card. They simply select their color and place it in the file. The color tells who has it, which is the most important piece of information.

- A check-out card policy must be included as company/department policy. No exceptions. No exemptions. Everyone must participate regardless of rank, position or length of time that the files are needed. If not, the system breaks down, files will once again be missing in action, and time will be wasted searching for files.

Whichever method you choose, be it an out log or check-out cards, these systems are critical to the continued success of your filing system.

Create a Disaster Recovery Plan

No matter where you live or conduct business, a disaster recovery plan is a must. It is the key to continuing your business even in the event of an emergency. While earthquakes, tornados and hurricanes tend to strike in specific parts of the country, fires, floods, and other disasters strike anywhere. Everyone must be prepared — both in the workplace and at home — with a disaster recovery plan.

FACT: Sixty-five percent of all businesses that suffer a disaster go out of business within 18 months due to an inadequate (or nonexistent) disaster recovery plan.

Records that are vital to the continuation of business include, but are not necessarily limited to:

1. Tax records

2. Legal documents

3. Insurance policies

4. Warranties

5. Financial records

6. Personnel records

Please note that categories 1-5 also apply to your home and personal records.

Storing these items only at the office is not adequate to prepare for an emergency. It is crucial that you make back-up copies (paper or computer disks on tape) and store them off-site. Many feel that having these items in a fireproof safe or vault is adequate on-site, and in some cases it is. But you must also consider an emergency where you may be unable to access the safe, get into the building, or where the building may not exist after the disaster. The safest plan is to send the back-up paper and computer files off-site.

Off-Site Storage

Many organizations lease space off-site, often in another city or state to house the back-up records. Particularly in areas that are prone to disasters, it's important to choose a site that would not be affected by the same disaster. Don't store the back-ups next door. For example: Los Angeles is prone to earthquakes. If your business were in Los Angeles, your off-site storage should be away from the immediate area, preferably in a non-earthquake-prone location.

To prepare, follow these steps:

- Decide which records are vital to your organization.

- Select a location for storage.

- Back-up paper and computer files.

- Prepare a written plan that clearly explains where the back-ups are stored and who is authorized to retrieve them.

- Train staff members about the written plan.

- Continue to update the vital records. The rule of thumb on how often to refresh the vital records back-up items is to ask yourself the following question: "How much and what information am I willing to do without or to recreate?" If several months lapse between back-ups, then you must be willing to recreate or do without all data that occurred in those months. Ask this question often to help motivate you to continue to update the disaster recovery plan.

Additional Disaster Recovery Considerations

- If you had only 15 minutes to prepare for a disaster, what would you gather?

  Ask this question for both the workplace and home. People who have lost their homes to disaster indicate that the most difficult items to replace are photographs and personal memorabilia. Gather those items into a central area so that if time is short, you can quickly grab them. Also create back-ups and use off-site storage for vital items when possible.

SUPER TIP!

For photographs:

- Store the photo negatives off-site. Place in a safe deposit box or send to a trusted friend or family member. Cost is minimal with this method.

- When you take film in to be developed, ask if your developer can place your photographs on a diskette in addition to creating prints. Many developers offer this feature for a minimal additional cost. Place the diskette in a safe deposit box or other off-site location as a disaster recovery tool. If needed, the photos from the diskette can be loaded onto a computer, viewed, cropped, and printed.

- Prepare to identify yourself and your medical insurance coverage and policy number if you or a family member required medical treatment. Could you quickly contact your insurance company with your policy number and know what your coverage is?

  IMPORTANT: Keep copies of household insurance policies off-site. If you need to contact your insurance company to process a claim, not only will you have the number, you will know what your coverage is and have the paperwork to prove it.

- If you needed cash after a disaster, what methods do you have at your disposal (checks, ATM) and how would you identify yourself?

SUPER TIP!

Keep a certain amount of cash on hand hidden in your home in case of emergency. Remember that many banks, ATMs and computers can be inaccessible after a disaster. The amount of cash you store is up to you; it should be adequate to help you through a few days if access to a bank were not possible.

The choices you make about what to back-up and where to place them are among the most crucial decisions you will ever make. These decisions can affect you, your business and family for the rest of your life.

Establish a Records Retention Schedule

Every organization needs to create and maintain a records retention schedule to determine when documents can legally be destroyed. Requirements vary by industry and state. Equally important, is how the documents should be disposed. Should they be shredded, discarded or recycled? To determine the retention schedule, answer the following questions:

Records Retention Appraisal Guidelines

The following questions should be answered when appraising a record (document) to determine its retention schedule.

1. Is this record/document...
   [ ] The original, office record copy?   [ ] A copy of an original/office record?
   If it is a copy, where is the original?
   [ ] Institution   [ ] Other department (which) _____
   [ ] Government agency   [ ] Other _____

2. Is the information contained on the record/document obtainable elsewhere?
   _____

   How is it retained?
   _____

   Where and in what format?
   _____

3. Who uses the record?
   [ ] Analyst   [ ] Examiner
   [ ] Senior management   [ ] Only this department
   [ ] All of the above   [ ] Above

4. How often is it used?

[ ] One time   [ ] Monthly, quarterly

[ ] Once a year — at a specific time   [ ] Spontaneously as events occur

[ ] Other _____

5. How long will this document/record be needed?

[ ] Current monthly only   [ ] Current quarter

[ ] Current year   [ ] Current year + 1 year

[ ] Current year + 2 years   [ ] Current year + 3 years

[ ] Current year + 5-10 years

6. What is the purpose of this record/document? (Check all that apply.)

[ ] Gives dates, names, places of activity/event

[ ] Used as basis for future decisions

[ ] Documents results/resolutions

7. What information does the document provide?

[ ] Financial, statistical

[ ] Documents results; resolutions

[ ] Presents facts, information concerning activity

[ ] Other _____

8. What would happen if the document/record was destroyed?

_____

_____

Various resources are available for information specific to your industry and state.

For government organizations: Contact the local or state historical societies. They often provide guidelines and suggested time frames for records disposal as well as disposal methods.

Example of Retention Schedule for Government Documents:

Document	Government Schedule	Periodic, Perpetual or Permanent	Active/Inactive Archive/Disposal
Accident Reports	Two years after end of fiscal year	Perpetual	Inactive then disposal
Bids (unsuccessful)	Two years after end of letting of contract provided audited by auditor of state	Perpetual	Inactive then disposal
Job Descriptions	Until superseded or classification abolished	Periodic	Inactive then disposal
Contracts	15 years after expiration	Periodic	Archive then disposal
Case Files — Civil	26 years after verdict is returned	Periodic	Archive then disposal
Case Files — Criminial	Never — Historical	Permanent	Archive
Personnel Files	Until employee terminates. Microfilm, destroy paper	Permanent	Archive then disposal
Publications — Manuals, Newsletters, Rules, Regs.	Historical — Never	Permanent	Archive
Annual Budgets	Historical — Never	Permanent	Archive

For government and private industry:

- Association of Records Managers and Administrators (ARMA) 1-800-422-2762 http://www.arma.org/hq. Materials can be purchased from ARMA on creating and implementing a record retention schedule.

- Information Requirements Clearinghouse 1-303-721-7500 http://www.irch.com also has material for sale on creating and implementing a record retention schedule. Information Requirements Clearinghouse also offers consulting services. For a fee, a representative will analyze your organization's needs and create a customized retention schedule.

These steps will ensure that your filing system is understood, and continues to be used correctly. You worked very hard redoing the filing systems. Don't let it fall apart once it is in place.

Chapter 6 Summary

Once your filing system has been created (with all of the tools in Chapter 4) it is critically important to make sure everyone using the system understands it and keeps it going.

1. Create and maintain an index.

   The index is a list of folders and their locations. The index can be retrieved on the computer and searched to help you locate any folder — active, inactive, or archives — in 60 seconds or less.

2. Set guidelines.

   Guidelines are a must for every central filing system. All users must understand and comply with the list of rules. A filing system where people are doing what they please simply does not work.

3. Keep track of files with a check-out system.

   To keep files from disappearing from the file cabinet without a trace, use one of the two check-out methods:

   — The out log

   — The check-out card system

4. Create a disaster recovery plan.

   Critical for both office and home. Determine which records are vital, which could not be replaced and follow the steps to create the disaster recovery plan.

5. Establish a records retention schedule.

How long do you keep records and when and how can they be destroyed? The Record Retention Schedule answers these questions. Record retention requirements vary from industry to industry and state to state. Obtain detailed information for your industry and state before finalizing your schedule.

7 PAPER HANDLING FOR THE ORGANIZATIONALLY IMPAIRED: PHASE 1

Creating and maintaining a filing system are just two pieces of the organizational puzzle. Handling the day-to-day paper avalanche is an equally important challenge for many people. How about you?

1. Do you have stacks of paper on your desk?

2. Are there stacks of paper on every flat surface of your working space including the floor and chairs?

3. Have you ever missed a deadline because you forgot a project was due?

4. Are you sometimes late for meetings because you can't find the items required for that meeting?

5. Do you go to other people to get copies of papers that you already have, but are buried somewhere in your office?

6. Has your "to be filed" stack become the "Leaning Tower of Pisa"?

7. Do you keep papers "just because"?

If you answered yes to at least three of these questions, you may consider yourself organizationally impaired. Organizational impairment although debilitating, is not a permanent and irreversible condition. Recovery is possible.

Let's begin with controlling paper as it comes to you. You've no doubt heard that you should handle each piece of paper only one time. That would be great in the perfect world, but in the real world there are many reasons an item can't be acted on right away.

- You need to take care of this item today, but right now are working on another higher priority project.

- You begin to work on the item but are interrupted and something else takes priority.

- You are waiting for feedback from someone else to complete a job.

- The item does not need to be done today. Maybe it's an item for tomorrow, or next week, or next month.

- This piece of paper is to be filed, but you can't go over to the cabinet and file it at this moment.

While it is unrealistic to expect to handle each item only once, you can decrease your clutter and stacks by organizing your office space and desk to create a place for every piece of paper as it comes to you.

The technique used to do this is called RAFT. Each letter in RAFT represents one of the four things that you can do with any piece of paper as it comes to you.

RAFT

- **R** oute or Refer

- **A** ct on it

- **F** ile it

- **T** oss (or recycle) it

RAFT

R oute or Refer

Look at each item that you receive to determine if it really is for you to act on. It may be something that you can pass along or route to someone else. Just because your name is on it does not mean you must take ownership of it.

RAFT

A ct

Many of the items that come to you really are for your attention; they require some action on your part. But perhaps you are working on something else at the moment or this action item does not require attention until later.

Does this scenario sound familiar? An item comes to you and you think, "I can't act on this now," and place it on a stack of other papers on the desk. Later in the day you shuffle through the same stack, rereading and reevaluating the items, often with the same reaction, "I can't act on this now," and back on the stack it goes. This scene is played over and over again throughout the day. Studies show that the average person will handle and rehandle the same item eight to ten times before acting on it. What a complete waste of time and brainpower!

The premise of time management is to cut down on this wasteful activity. Whereas handling an item only once may not be reasonable in the real world, handling the item eight to ten times is an outrageous waste. Two simple organizing systems can be used to place these items in the proper place for efficient handling:

- Tickler system: A place to put items to be acted on in the future (any time other than today).

- Today organizer: A place to put items to be acted on some time today.

Tickler System

The most important thing is to place the tickler close to your chair in your work area. It needs to be within arm's reach so you don't have to get up out of your chair to access it. You will be using the tickler all day, every day. Remember the adage "Usage Determines Storage" so place it close at hand.

The most common place for a tickler system is in the left- or right-hand drawer of your desk. However, you will also find other kinds of desktop tickler systems at the office supply store. Two popular prefabricated types are:

- An expanding accordion file where slots are set up 1-31, representing the days of the month. Optionally, this can be used along with another accordion file where slots are designated for the months of the year, January through December.

- A book-style tickler that has slots for 1-31 between covers. This type has just the 1-31 for the days of the month or has added slots for the months January through December.

Which type of tickler would be best for you? If you spend all your time at the office, then any method will work well for you. If you are frequently out of the office, you might consider the accordion or book-style tickler due to their portability.

If you choose to set up the tickler in the desk drawer, you need these supplies:

- Thirty-one hanging Pendaflex™ type folders with tabs attached to the front numbered 1-31.

SUPER TIP!

Hanging folders are also available that are closed on the ends creating an envelope effect. This is very useful for a tickler system because items cannot fall out of the sides of the folder.

- If you use a standard hanging file folder (open on the ends) you may want to place a file jacket inside each hanging folder. This creates the envelope effect so that items don't fall out of the sides.

Each of these folders represents a day of the month. Place the folder for the current date in the front of the drawer. For example, if today were September 8, you place the folder with the tab for the eighth in the front of the drawer. All others fall behind in numerical order.

Using the Tickler System

An item comes to you and your response is "I can't act on this now; it's for tomorrow," and you place the item in the folder for tomorrow (September 9). As other items come to you, determine when they need to be acted on and place them in the appropriate folder.

SUPER TIP!

Don't drop the item into the folder for the day the item is due. Give yourself several extra days before due dates. This is the most realistic way to plan for the unexpected.

You might also place 11 more hanging folders in the drawer in addition to the 1-31. These represent the months of the year and are useful for items beyond the current month. This is great for all of those items that you just don't know what to do with because they are for so far into the future.

At the end of a working day, today's folder must be empty. You will then physically lift the hanging folder out of the drawer and move it to the back, pushing tomorrow's folder forward. With this technique, today's folder is always in the front of the drawer regardless of what day it is. The benefit is that you don't have to continually ask yourself what the date is. Just open the drawer and today is in the front.

At the beginning of any month, empty the new month's folder and disseminate the contents into the 1-31 daily folders. Remember that you have been collecting items in the monthly folder for the past 11 months. Some of the items are to be acted on at the beginning of the month, some for the middle and some for the end.

SUPER TIP!

If you use monthly folders in addition to the daily folders, when you lift today's folder to move it back, move it behind next month's folder. For example, at the end of the day on September 1, lift and move the folder back behind October's folder. The next time that the first of the month will occur will be in October, so as the daily folders are pushed back, the October folder continues to move forward and all days behind it now represent the first, second, etc. of October.

SUPER TIP!

At the beginning of a new month, use a paper clip to close off folders for days that you will not be there. Do this for weekends, holidays, vacation days or any day that you will be out of the office. Now you cannot accidentally drop an item into a folder for a day that you will not be there.

SUPER TIP!

When placing items into a monthly folder, make notations in the upper-right corner of the date that the item needs to be acted on. Use a small yellow sticky if you prefer not to write directly on the item. With this technique, when you disseminate the items from the monthly folder into the days of the new month, it will take far less reading and evaluating time.

SUPER TIP!

If you handle paperwork for more than just yourself, you don't need multiple tickler systems. Use one tickler system and color-coding to quickly determine which items belong to whom. Color-coded removable dots are perfect for this. Place the dot in the upper-right corner of the document. For example, if you work with Bob and Yolanda, use blue color-coded removable dots for Bob and yellow color-coded removable dots for Yolanda. The color quickly signals to your brain who the item is for.

SUPER TIP!

If you frequently need tickler items before the due dates, keep a log on your computer of tickler items. Create a document called Tickler and as items are placed into the tickler, make a note of it on the computer. If you need an item, you can search for it and the tickler computer file will tell you which folder the item is in.

The category headings for the tickler document will be according to how you will look for items. For example, do you use document names or numbers? Will you look for it by project title? Or who it is for? Consider these questions to help you decide on appropriate headings for the tickler document.

If you prefer not to use the computer, you can track tickler items on a calendar or in a logbook also allowing you to search for particular items before their tickler dates.

SUPER TIP!

You must look at the tickler on a daily basis. If a few days go by without checking the tickler, items will slip by undone and there can be some very negative results. Studies show that we can develop a habit by doing a behavior for 21 to 23 days, so put a notation on your calendar to check the tickler for 23 days. By day 24, you will be in the habit of checking the tickler system.

The tickler is the first of the "I can't act on it now" techniques, a place to put items to be acted on in the future. But what about all of the items that come to you during the day that are not for the future, but are for today. The second "I can't act on it now" technique is a today organizer.

Today Organizer

One way to really cut down on the handling and rehandling of items is to place an organizer on your desk for items to be acted on today. With the today organizer, each place has meaning so that you do much less reading and reevaluating of items.

Each slot of the organizer will have meaning according to the way you work. For example, you may have slots set up by:

- Priority — high, medium and low

- Project — a slot for project X, project Y, project Z

- Person — a slot for Gerry, Sam and Harvey

Let's use priority as an example of how the today organizer works:

1. As items come to you, read and determine the importance of each item. You know that this is something you can't act on now, but need to act on today.

2. Determine how important the today item is. Is this a high, medium or low priority item for today?

3. Place it into the high, medium or low priority slot of the today organizer.

When you are ready to move on to the next today item, you can reach right to the most important items first. They are right there on your desk, already in a designated spot. No need to read and evaluate everything in the stack just to determine what needs to be done next. The today organizer already does that for you.

What does the today organizer look like?

Go to the office supply store or look in the supply catalog for File Organizers or Step-File Organizers. These are customarily made of metal or coated metal and generally have seven to eleven compartments which hold papers vertically rather than horizontally. Be sure that the compartments are of adequate size for holding papers; some organizers are made specifically for organizing envelopes and are too small for this purpose. *The today organizer is not to be used as a storage unit.* Every item in it is to be acted on today. Remember, if it is an item for the future, it is placed in the tickler system.

> ### SUPER TIP!
>
> Be sure to place the today organizer close at hand and in your line of vision from your chair. When you see these items in the today organizer, it will prompt you to act on them.

Can I use stacking trays instead of the organizer?

No. For people who are "paper stackers," stacking trays can be a trap. Stacking trays simply create elevated stacks of paper. As soon as a piece of paper is placed in the tray, it becomes the beginning of a new stack, and is stored there until desk clean-up day. Stacking trays also often result in constant paper searching, shuffling and missed deadlines. If you are a paper stacker, do not use stacking trays.

Between the tickler system and the today organizer, the stacks of paper on your desk are already diminishing. Continue to use these techniques on a daily basis and you will see the results in less clutter, fewer stacks and greater ease in putting your hands on documents quickly.

RA**F**T

F ile It

Many "to be filed" items come to you on a daily basis. If you can't file the item right away, you have two options:

1. **Have a "to be filed" holder at your desk.** A "to be filed" bin on top of the file cabinet is fine for people to share, but you must also have your own "to be filed" physically close to you. If you only use the "to be filed" over on the file cabinet, and you don't have time to file the item now, how will you have the time to get up and place the item in the "to be filed"? Remember, "Usage Determines Storage." You use the "to be filed" all day, so it should be close to you.

2. **Prefile.** Rather than using a "to be filed" bin, derive benefit from each time you handle an item by prefiling. For example, if you file alphabetically, use an accordion file already labeled A-Z as the "to be filed." Prefile items in the appropriate slot.

When you are ready to file, take the accordion file to the file cabinet with you. Filing will be much quicker because it is already in order.

> ### SUPER TIP!
>
> If your filing system is other than an alphabetical system, (remember SPACNG) you can change the labels on the accordion file to match your system. Whether you use an accordion file or some other method, be sure that you design it to always derive benefit from each time you handle an item.

RAF<u>T</u>

T oss It (or Recycle)

Have both a wastebasket and a recycle bin close at hand and be sure to use them. If this is particularly hard for you, be sure to read Chapter 9, Letting Paper Go: The 12-Step Recovery Program.

Follow RAFT and your desk will be significantly less cluttered and more organized — making you significantly more productive.

Chapter 7 Summary

Adopt RAFT to help you get a handle on paper as it comes to you. Granted, you may handle some items more than once, but you will derive some benefit from each time you do handle it.

1. **Route or Refer.** Route the paper to someone else.

2. **Act on it.** Place it into the tickler system for tomorrow and beyond. Place it into the today organizer for items to be acted on today.

3. **File it.** Use prefiling to organize paper before it is filed. Keep the prefiling tool, such as an accordion file, close at hand at your desk.

4. **Toss it or recycle.** Do just that. If it is an item that can be disposed of, do it.

8 PAPER HANDLING FOR THE ORGANIZATIONALLY IMPAIRED: PHASE 2

Letting Paper Go — The 12-Step Recovery Program

RAFT is designed to give you a place for each and every piece of paper that comes your way. However, many people keep many more items than needed. If you hang onto everything, you may be considered a Packrat.

Packrats tend to have difficulty getting rid of anything. When assessing an item such as a piece of paper (or e-mail message) the Packrat will generally keep the item because someday they might need it or want it. Then the Packrat is faced with what to do with the item, where to put it, how to find it again, and how long to keep it.

The following 12 questions are ones that you will ask yourself for each item that comes to you. If you cannot give good legitimate answers to these questions, let it go, toss or recycle.

1. Why do I need it?

2. Why do I want it?

3. Why is it significant?

4. How will it be used now or in the future?

5. Is it information that I already have in another file?

6. Is it quality information?

7. Is the information accurate and reliable?

8. Is it timely?

9. What is the lifespan of this item? Long-term or short-term?

10. Can I obtain the information from another source?

11. Will others come to me for this item?

12. What is the worst thing that could happen to me if I get rid of this item?

Now, let's get further perspective on this list:

- **Questions 1 - 4.** Why do I need it? Why do I want it? Why is it significant? How will it be used now or in the future? Notice that the words "why" and "how" create real meaning in these questions. Many Packrats indicate that they keep items "just because" or say "but I might need or want this," without giving a reason. "Why" forces you to give an answer to this item's importance. If you can't give a reason why you need it, want it, what its significance is or what you are going to do with it, get rid of it.

- **Question 5.** Is it information that I already have in another file? If the item is already filed elsewhere, do not file it again. Use one of the two cross-referencing techniques (simple cross-referencing or the cross-reference sheet) then get rid of the duplicate copy.

- **Questions 6 - 8.** Is it quality information? Is the information accurate and reliable? Is it timely? It is not uncommon for people to hang on to a lot of old information that is no longer quality, accurate or timely. How many times have you gone through the file cabinet only to find items, such as an inter-office memo that says "Reminder of staff meeting next week" and the item is three years old. This is a perfect example of an item that is no longer quality, accurate or timely. Get rid of it.

  If the reminder memo is still current, it's a perfect candidate for the tickler system. When the date for the staff meeting comes and goes, the memo can be discarded. This kind of memo will no longer be filed in the file cabinet at all.

If you do have these old items in the file cabinet, be sure to follow the Document Life Cycle reviewing the active file cabinets once a year. Remember, the first time that you go through the active cabinets it will be necessary to review each document in each folder. This is exactly the kind of item you are looking for.

- **Question 9.** What is the lifespan of this item? Long-term or short-term? If this is a short-term item, it is placed either in the tickler system or today organizer. If it is a long-term item, it is filed in the filing system.

- **Question 10.** Can I obtain the information from another source?

Check the World Wide Web for online copies of catalogs, brochures and other dated materials. Many items that come routinely in the mail are also published on the Web. How do you know? Look for the Web address, which will always begin with "http://..." If you see that address, check the Web site to see how extensive and up-to-date the material is. Often times the information on the Web will be even more timely than the material you receive in the mail. If that is the case, toss/recycle all older materials, keeping only the most recent version. Then continue to watch the Web site for changes and new information.

Can you obtain the information from the originator? For example, when you receive inter-office material, do you really need to keep it? Is it for you to act on? Does it have any real importance or significance to you? Or, is this material just for your information?

If it is only for your information, toss/recycle and if you really needed the item again obtain it from the originator. If you are concerned that the originator may not have the item when you need it, ask yourself this question: "If this item was not important enough for the originator to keep, is it important enough for me to keep?" That question can offer perspective on the importance and significance of the item.

- **Question 11.** Will others come to me for this item? If you are the person that everyone comes to for items, it could be that you keep this item for no other reason. You don't need it, use it, or want it, but others will come to you when they need it. This is reason enough to keep the item.

SUPER TIP!

If you are keeping this item for no other reason other than people will come to you for it, be sure to place it in a central location that others have access to. Do not keep these items in your working space. Keeping it in your working space only guarantees that you will be interrupted when someone needs the item. Why should you be interrupted for items that you have no use for? Don't take ownership of items that you don't need or use.

- **Question 12.** What is the worst thing that could happen to me if I get rid of this item? This is perhaps the most important question of all. The other 11 steps of the 12-step program are designed to help you let go of as much paper as possible. However, in the real world, there are sometimes consequences for getting rid of items we should not have. If the worst thing that happens to you is that you obtain the item from another source, that's not so bad. Get rid of it. If the worst thing that happens to you is that you are reprimanded or another more severe penalty, then keep it. Follow the tip for question 11 of keeping these items in a central area where others can obtain them if necessary.

The more difficult it is for you to get rid of paper, the more important it is that you review each of the 12-step questions for every item that comes your way. Combine the 12-step program with RAFT and you have much less paper cluttering your office space.

Filing: When to Get It Done

The challenge for many is the self-discipline to keep filing under control, to not let stacks and stacks of "to be filed" grow and take over the office. Remember that filing is critical to the success of your organization. Records and materials must be complete at all times.

The goal is to get into the habit of filing on a daily basis. This is really much easier than it sounds using the following two techniques:

File Daily

Technique #1 — Select a certain time of the day to do the daily filing. The time doesn't necessarily have to be a time on the clock, it can be:

- Every afternoon before you leave the office

- Every morning when you first come in

- Every day when you return from lunch

- When co-workers or supervisors are out of the office so you won't be interrupted

- During your low energy time of the day. For most people that time is 3:00 p.m. Once your filing system is in place daily, filing won't take a lot of brain power and is a perfect thing to do when you have difficulty concentrating on other tasks.

Technique #2 — Designate a certain amount of time to devote to the daily filing. The time limit means that even if you do not finish in the designated time, the task is still done for the day. It becomes a game that you play with yourself to see how much you really can do in that 10 or 15 minutes. You will determine the amount of time according to how much daily filing you have.

The good news is that in most business situations, daily filing per person can be done in 10 minutes a day or less. If you use the prefiling technique from RAFT, your filing will be even faster because it will already be in order. There are exceptions to this 10-minute rule, of course. Often times medical offices or law offices are exceptions. If you consider in a medical office that every patient chart must be refiled every day, this can often times take one to two hours a day.

Make notations on your calendar for the first 21 to 23 days to file daily. It will take 21 to 23 days for daily filing to become a habit. Some of those days, you may not be thrilled that you made the commitment; but stay with it. By day 24, filing every day will be part of your routine, just like checking voice mail or e-mail every morning or any other task that you do every day.

What about the stacks of "to be filed" that are waiting to be done?

Many people wait for the stacks of "to be filed" to get out of control, then go into the office on a weekend to get the quantity filing done in a filing marathon. This is a temporary solution that does not help you learn any good new habits. Like weeds in a garden, four or five days later, the stacks will sprout up again.

The most important thing is to get into the habit of filing daily. During those first 23 days, leave the stacks of "to be filed" right where they are. Don't bother with them for the time being. On day 24, go over to the "to be filed" stack and pull a few items off the top and file them along with your daily filing. Each day select a few more items. Little by little, the stacks will diminish. Will this technique take time? Yes, indeed it will, but the long-term benefit of keeping up with the filing from this time forward will far outweigh a weekend filing marathon.

In Pursuit of the Paperless Office

You've heard of the paperless office, but have you seen it? The promise of technology has been that files, records and documents would be stored on computer and the need for hard copies would be eliminated. This is true for storage of some documents, but also true is that with the availability of computers with printers, photocopiers, fax machines and other technologies, we often create more paper than necessary.

Where the paperless office may not be a reality, the paperless office is possible by following these techniques:

- **Will this be stored as a computer file OR on paper?** Decide whether a particular document is going to be stored on the computer or on paper. Even though computers have the capacity to store and retrieve files at will, many people will print and file a document that is already on the computer. This is a waste of paper, file cabinet space and your filing time. If the document is stored on the computer, you can always print it out at a later time if needed.

  Exceptions to this rule are:

  1. Items with handwritten notes or signatures, such as contracts. Yes, you will have them on the computer system and you will also have the hard copy stored in the file cabinet.

  2. Items that you are required to keep as a hard copy. Many industries such as government and law enforcement environments require that certain items be kept as paper. Legal requirements are always an exception to the computer or paper rule.

  3. A file that must be complete at all times, for example, a client file in a legal environment. It would not be proper for a client folder to not be complete at all times.

Many people would like to keep only the computer version of a file, but they either don't trust the computer or they don't trust themselves to find the file when it is needed. It's important that you don't trust only one copy of a file on the computer. Hard drives crash, networks go down, disasters occur. This is why it is of critical importance that computer files be backed-up.

If you are working on a Local Area Network (LAN), the network administrator is responsible for backing up the shared network drives. But the network administrator is not necessarily required to back-up your individual hard drive, usually referred to as the "C" drive. Check with the network administrator of your office to find out what is or is not being backed-up and for recommendations of back-up methods. Should you create back-ups onto diskettes, tape, etc.?

If you don't trust yourself to find the file in short order when it is needed, be sure to spend time creating clear, logical directories and subdirectories for your hard drive. Once you really have a handle on this, you will be able to put your hands on any computer document in 60 seconds or less, eliminating the need for the paper version.

- **Use e-mail whenever possible**. Use e-mail to distribute inter-office communications. Not only does this cut back dramatically on the amount of paper generated and distributed, it also cuts back on the amount of paper subsequently filed repeatedly within the organization.

Let's say you distribute an inter-office memo to 100 people. That is a guarantee of 100 sheets of paper used. Then each of the 100 people will question whether they need to file this item. Even if only 50 percent of people file this, the same item has now been filed 50 times within the organization. Space costs money. This is an enormous waste of both space and money.

Using e-mail for inter-office distribution dramatically cuts the paper and filing of this item. Suggest this as a policy for your organization. The e-mail method works beautifully except when people print every e-mail.

- **Be selective about which e-mail messages to print**. Try not to print e-mail messages unless truly necessary. Many of the e-mails we receive are F.Y.I or For Your Information messages. Read each message twice to determine if it's something that you must have as a hard copy. If it's an item that you can note on your calendar, do so rather than printing.

- **Print on both sides of the paper**. This is a great technique to cut back on the paper generated when creating draft versions of documents. When a document is printed the first time, it is rarely perfect. A word is misspelled, a comma is missing or the content needs to be changed. This piece of paper is now wasted. Put that same piece of paper back into the printer tray and print on the backside for another draft. When both sides are used, recycle it.

  This method is not recommended if you share a printer with other people or the printer is not logistically close to you. Your co-workers are not likely to fully appreciate your paper saving methods when they are trying to get a document printed and your draft is on the backside.

- **Do you need to be on all of these distribution lists?** Analyze each distribution list that you are on. If you find that you routinely pass items on to the next person on the list without reviewing it first, or distribution items stack up unread or unreviewed, you may not really need to be on that list at all.

- **Eliminate fax cover sheets whenever possible.**

- **Use the photocopier sparingly.**

- **Make notes on the calendar; get rid of the paper**. If the calendar notation is enough, get rid of the paper. If the paper is also necessary, place it in the tickler system as well as noting the item on the calendar.

> **SUPER TIP!**
>
> Next to appointments that also have an item in the tickler system, write a "T" and circle it on the calendar. When you look at the item on the calendar and see the "T," you know to retrieve the corresponding item from the tickler system.

Chapter 8 Summary

1. Let paper go by using the 12-Step Recovery Program.

   Review the 12 questions for each piece of paper that comes your way. Determine the item's importance and whether it should be kept or not. Then determine where kept items should be placed, in the today organizer, the tickler system or in the file cabinet.

2. File daily using the techniques that successful daily filers use.

   • Select a certain time of the day to do daily filing.

   • Select a certain amount of time to devote to daily filing.

   • Commit to daily filing for 23 days and it becomes a habit. Just another item in the daily routine.

3. Create the paperless office.

   • Will this be stored as a computer file or paper? Store a particular document either on the computer or as paper. Do not keep both for the same document. Review the exceptions to this rule.

   • Use e-mail whenever possible. This not only eliminates paper from being generated to begin with, but then lessens the amount of times that the same document will be filed repeatedly within the organization.

- Be selective about which e-mail messages to print. Lots of items received in e-mail are just for your information. Look twice at e-mail messages to determine if printing is truly necessary.

- Print on both sides of paper for drafts. This technique cuts way down on the amount of paper used.

- Remove yourself from distribution lists wherever possible.

- Eliminate fax cover sheets.

- Use the photocopier sparingly.

- Make a notation on your calendar as a reminder rather than keeping all related papers.

9 OPTIMIZE SPACE AND TIME

Space and time are two things we just never have enough of. Optimizing both will increase your every day effectiveness tremendously.

Inbox

The placement of your inbox can have a tremendous effect on your time and space efficiency. If your inbox is on your desk, do you:

- Find yourself looking at the inbox every time something is dropped in?

- Use the inbox as a storage bin, stacking items you need to do?

- Find that junk mail seems to overflow from the inbox and onto your desk?

If so, move the inbox as far away from your desk as possible to minimize the number of times you are interrupted during the day. Put it just outside (or inside) your doorway and check it only at scheduled times throughout the day. Workdays are already filled with telephone and in-person interruptions, but interrupting yourself to look at something unrelated to the task at hand is a monumental waste of time and energy. If you find yourself drawn to looking at the inbox every time something is dropped in, move it.

Place the following items near your inbox:

- Outbox

- Inter-office envelopes

- Trash basket

- Recycle bin

Go to the inbox at specified intervals during the day, and sort through the mail while standing in the hallway. Remember RAFT.

Anything that can be routed or referred to someone else, put right into an inter-office envelope and directly into the outbox. Items that can be tossed or recycled are disposed of right there in the hallway. The only items that come through your doorway and into your workspace are items for you to act on which are immediately put in the tickler or today organizer, and items to be filed which are placed in the "to be filed" accordion file.

Moving the inbox not only lessens the number of interruptions that we impose on ourselves, it minimizes the amount of clutter that ever reaches the desk.

Reading Materials — Catalogs, Brochures, Magazines and Trade Journals

These are the items that take up the most office space and require the most time to go through. And they just keep coming. If you ever begin to catch up, the next batch arrives and buries you once again.

Keep in mind that catalogs, brochures, magazines and trade journals are dated materials with a finite lifespan. The best way to begin organizing these items is to dispose of the ones that are too outdated to be of value.

Coping with Catalogs and Brochures

Keep only the latest version and toss/recycle all older ones. While it is true that items offered change from time to time, items not listed in the newer version are typically no longer available. Toss/recycle the old version before filing the new one.

Smaller catalogs and brochures can be filed in a file cabinet drawer. Consider a magazine box for larger catalogs. Organizing them is your next challenge.

- Will you think of them according to the type of item you see in the catalog/brochure, for example, office supplies?

- Will you look for it by the vendor name?

- Should they be stored in your desk drawer or across the room in the file cabinet?

- Do you use them often?

- Do people come to you for the information contained in the brochure or catalog?

The more often you access them, the closer to you they should be stored. Remember, "Usage Determines Storage."

Managing Magazines and Trade Journals

Lifespans vary by industry. Use two years as a maximum rule of thumb. Fast-paced, growing industries' materials (e.g., computer technology, Internet, etc.) will be outdated much more quickly. Magazines and trade journals are designed to give you the latest, most recent information available. Keep pace with your industry and toss/recycle outdated materials.

SUPER TIP!

Check the World Wide Web on the Internet for the catalogs, brochures, magazines and trade journals you need. The Web is a great place to check the latest and greatest information offered giving you more freedom to toss/recycle the hard copies or to cancel your subscription altogether.

SUPER TIP!

Donate appropriate magazines to medical offices, your local library, hospitals or home for the aged; these will be greatly appreciated. No matter how old the magazines are, if they contain pictures, they can be donated to an elementary school. The children can always cut out the pictures for school projects.

Magazine boxes found in office supply stores are a great way to store these items. The items are stored vertically eliminating the stacks, and making titles easy to read. To determine storage per box decide if you look for it by the name of the magazine/trade journal or if you will look for it by the month of publication. Place them in boxes accordingly. File by magazine titles, such as grouping Architectural Digest or all Internet World together, or by month, i.e., all January issues together, all February, etc.

Where you store the boxes will be based on how frequently you use the contents and how often others come to you for the magazines and journals. The more often you access them, the closer to you they should be stored. Once again, Usage Determines Storage.

How to find articles again. Most people initially flip through a magazine to get an idea of what articles to go back to later. When later comes, they waste a great deal of time and energy trying to remember what magazine the article was in and in which issue. Try one of these techniques to reduce frustration and inefficiency. Adapt them to best suit your needs.

Article Technique #1

- Before placing the magazine into the box, photocopy the table of contents or index, whichever is most useful to you.

- Use a colored highlighter to mark the titles of the articles that you are interested in referring to later.

- Paper clip all of the tables of contents together for the magazines in a given box and place in the front of the box.

- Later, when you need a specific article, pull out and visually scan the photocopied tables of contents. You will see the highlighted article you want in the list, which then indicates in which issue the article will be found.

SUPER TIP!

Color-code the highlighters. Use different colors for different meanings. For example, if an article is business related, use blue. If the article is for your personal interest, use green.

Article Technique #2

Use color-coded sticky notes or flags in the magazine itself. Use different color stickies or flags for different meanings as described above. You can use Article Techniques 1 and 2 together. If so, be sure that you use the same colors to identify meanings.

Article Technique #3

Use positioning of sticky notes or flags (rather than color) in the magazine to indicate meaning (e.g., place the flag close to the binding of the magazine to indicate that the article is business-related; place it close to the outside edge of the page if article is for personal use).

Article Technique #4

Clip the article(s) you want rather than wasting space keeping the whole magazine, trade journal or newspaper. Note the source and date on the clipping.

Slide the clippings into plastic sheet protectors with a three-hole punch, and place them in binders. Just flip through the binder to locate the article when needed. As articles become outdated, toss/recycle and use the sheet protector again for another article.

SUPER TIP!

Color-code the binders according to topic.

Finding the Time to Read

Now that you have organized your reading material, how do you find the time to read it?

- Carry a "to be read" notebook with you at all times. Use waiting times as reading times. Read while waiting for a meeting to begin; a medical appointment — even while standing in lines. This is a great use of time.

- Only read what is important for you to read. Anything else, circulate to give others the opportunity to review.

- Keep pleasure reading where you can catch up with it at will.

Distribution Lists

Are you on so many inter-office distribution lists that you couldn't possibly read all of the material that comes your way? Do you route the unread items on to the next person just to get them off your desk? Is the inbox pile growing because you just can't keep up? Here are two techniques to pare this down.

1. Remove yourself from any distribution lists that you do not absolutely need to be part of. If you can find the information elsewhere — or if it just isn't important to you — have your name removed from the list.

2. Create a reading forum. To decrease the amount of reading, each person in the department is assigned one or two magazines/trade journals to read and review each month. That individual then writes up a summarized version of what they found to be useful in that particular issue and distributes it via e-mail to the other department members. Each person has access to the full-size article if they are interested in pursuing it on their own. A reading forum keeps everyone informed while minimizing the read time required of each individual. With each person being responsible for one or two issues, this cuts way back on the amount of reading that each and every person is required to do.

Calendars and Appointment Methods

A multitude of calendar and appointment schedulers are available. Select *one* that meets all your needs. Yes, one!

Do not keep a calendar on your desk, another in your briefcase and another on the refrigerator door. Keep one central calendar where all events are written to eliminate confusion and missed appointments or deadlines. If you keep multiple calendars and fail to write an appointment in one, it is inevitably the one you refer to when the day comes.

Exceptions to the one calendar rule are:

- Having a separate business and personal calendar. If you use a desk calendar and don't want others to see your personal appointments, keep them separate.

- If you keep calendars for different people, events or rooms. For example, if you are responsible for scheduling use of conference rooms, you would use a separate calendar from the one you use for your own appointments and meetings.

The biggest determining factor in which calendar to use is where you spend your time.

If you spend your time at a desk in the office, some optimal choices might be:

- Desk or wall calendar

- Computerized calendar software such as Schedule +, Lotus Organizer, Daytimer Organizer, Outlook, etc.

If you are in and out of the office, you might also consider:

- Calendar book that you carry with you such as a Franklin Covey Planner, Daytimer or Dayrunner. You can certainly use the calendar book as is, or use it with a corresponding software program which allows you to type your appointments, to-do lists, telephone book, etc. into the computer, then print out onto paper designed to fit in the calendar book. This makes the book neater and easier to read. When at your desk, just open the calendar book onto your desk for easy reference.

- Electronic handheld organizer such as the Sharp Wizard series. These are portable and keep track of your calendar, telephone book, to-do list, notes and memos, and more. Corresponding computer software allows you to enter all data onto your computer using a full-size keyboard, then transfer the data to the handheld organizer.

- Palmtop or handheld computers made by many major manufacturers such as Apple, Hewlett-Packard and more. These units typically have the calendar capabilities of electronic handheld organizers plus they accommodate scaled-down versions of popular software and operating systems, such as Windows 95™, Microsoft Word™ and Excel™ as well as an Internet browser.

This technology is changing and growing quickly. Consult the Internet, electronics stores, computer stores, and office supply stores for innovations as they occur.

Chapter 9 Summary

Your office can be organized to minimize clutter and lessen the number of interruptions. Get a handle on all of those "to be read" piles and never miss an appointment or a deadline.

Inbox

- Move the inbox as far from your desk as possible to reduce interruptions and clutter.

- Team the inbox with the outbox, inter-office envelopes, trash basket and recycle bin.

- Check the inbox at certain times of the day.

Reading Materials — Catalogs, Brochures, Magazines and Trade Journals

- Toss/Recycle or donate items that are two years or older.

- Store them in magazine boxes according to "Usage Determines Storage."

- Use color-coding to help you find articles again.

- Tear out articles of interest and place in plastic sheet protectors in color-coded binders.

- Remove yourself from unnecessary distribution lists.

- Create a reading forum. Each member of the team is responsible for reading certain materials and sharing the highlights with the other members of the team.

Calendars and Appointment Methods

- Keep only one calendar.

- Select the calendar method according to your work style—in the office or on the go.

10 THE FIVE KEYS TO ORGANIZATIONAL SUCCESS

Five standard techniques are used by successful organizers. (Remember that they were not born with the "organizational gene" or sprinkled with magic dust — they simply use these five techniques.)

Key 1. Assess — Evaluate the Current System

As discussed in Chapter 3, successful organizers are constantly assessing and reassessing the current system to be sure that it is accurate and up-to-date. Here are the questions to ask when evaluating any system.

- Does it work? Can I find what I'm looking for? Is it logical?

- Do I like it? Do I like the system as it is today? Is it physically convenient? Do the headings on folders, etc. make sense?

- Where do I spend my time? Different storage decisions are needed depending on where you spend your business time. Are you in the office most of the time? Are you an "on the go, on the run" kind of person who conducts business from the car or at other facilities?

- Does it work for others? If you are sharing information and files with other people, ask questions 1, 2 and 3 on their behalf.

Key 2. Make Appointments With Yourself

How likely are you to walk into the office one morning and say, "Gee, today seems like a good day to go through the active file cabinets, and separate the inactives and archives." That's why scheduling these tasks is so important. Select a date and time(s) when you are least likely to be interrupted. Is your firm quieter around the holidays? A certain day of the week? Around the lunch hour? Choose a date and time, mark it on your calendar and stick with it.

SUPER TIP!

Appointments don't have to be for an entire day or morning. Schedule short bursts of time — whatever you think you can manage and stick with. You will be amazed at how much you can accomplish in 20 minutes. When the time is up, note exactly where you left off and move on to the other items on your calendar or to-do list. Be sure to make and keep enough appointments to finish the job!

Key 3. Daily To-Do List

Use the daily to-do list with your tickler system and appointment schedule to be completely clear about what is to be accomplished during the day. Without the to-do list, it is easy to waste the day with tasks that occur on a whim, or to spend the entire day putting out fires — then wonder what happened to the day. The to-do list keeps you focused on the important tasks.

SUPER TIP!

Take five minutes at the end of each workday to review what was accomplished from that day's to-do list and carry over unfinished items to the next day's list. Add any follow-up phone calls, projects to be started and items from your calendar or tickler system to prepare for a "running start" the next morning.

Most people need 15 minutes each morning to reacquaint themselves with where they left off the afternoon before and to decide on that day's tasks. By taking five minutes at the end of each workday — while the tasks are fresh on your mind — you save that 15 minutes each morning. That's a total of 1 hour and 15 minutes of better utilized time each week — which translates into a full work week gained each year!

SUPER TIP!

Prioritize the to-do list with "A," "B" or "C" items with "A" items being the most important and "C" items being least important. Should the "A" items always be done first? Not necessarily. Use Key 4 as your guide.

Key 4. "What Is the Best Use of My Time Right Now?"

Ask yourself this question throughout the day to determine which tickler, appointment or to-do list item you should do based on your energy and attention level at any given time.

Everyone has high and low energy times of the day. High energy time for most people is at 10:30 a.m.; lowest ebb of energy is typically at 3:00 p.m. Generally, high-energy time should be focused on "A" (most important) items. "C" items can be done at your lowest energy period; they usually don't require the same amount of concentration and attention to detail as the "A" items.

Key 5. Do It!

You can assess, plan, put the task on a calendar, put it on the to-do list, but nothing happens until you do it. Whatever task you have been putting off, just get in there and do it. Schedule it in short bursts so it isn't overwhelming. Commit to it—and do it! You'll be glad you did.

Chapter 10 Summary

Use the Five Keys to Organizational Success on a daily basis.

- Assess

- Make Appointments With Yourself

- Daily To-Do List

- "What Is the Best Use of My Time Right Now?"

- Do It!

11 ORGANIZATIONAL QUICKTIPS

Organizational Quicktips

- Keep office supplies close at hand — especially those needed to create new files.

- Create only one to-do list per day.

- Plan travel time realistically. Don't keep others waiting.

- Take your "to be read" file with you in case you are the one kept waiting.

- Prepare for any project the afternoon/evening before. Set out all of the tools and supplies so when you arrive in the morning, you are ready to go.

- Cruise the aisles of the office supply stores to stay abreast of the latest tools.

- Delegate whenever possible.

- Create a central place at home for schoolbooks, homework, library books, etc., so you don't have to search the house daily.

- In a two-story house, have a spot on each level for items that need to be carried up or down. Never waste a trip.

- Leave reminder messages on your own voice mail/answering machine.

- Use the phone instead of writing out replies.

- Eliminate negative self-talk. The more you say you hate filing, the more you will hate filing.

- Cancel any subscriptions that you don't have time to read.

- Carry postcards, stationery and blank greeting cards with you so you can quickly write notes while waiting for appointments, flights, etc.

- Keep one phone list. Use the same guidelines as choosing a calendar method. Where do you spend your time?

- Interview other successful organizers. Find out what techniques they use and adapt them to your needs.

- Learn speed reading. Take a course, read a book or listen to speed reading tapes.

- When leaving a voice mail message always leave your phone number. Don't assume the person has it with them or that it is easily accessible.

- Don't file envelopes.

- Learn the shortcuts of your computer software. Take a course, get a book or video. Think of the time wasted doing computer tasks the long way.

- Select one place for keys, receipts and money in your briefcase or purse. No more searching. Spending 10 minutes a day searching for misplaced items wastes 60 hours a year.

- Keep only the business cards that you think you will use or follow-up on. There is no law against throwing away a business card.

- Use binders for items that are updated frequently or that need to be portable. Binders are easier to carry to a meeting than file folders.

- Strengthen you memory skills. Read a book or listen to memory tapes.

- If you are right-handed, place the phone on the left side. If you are left-handed, reverse.

- Place event or airline tickets in the tickler. File them according to date a couple of days before the event.

- Apply all of the organizing techniques learned in this book to your home. Closets, kitchen, linen cabinets. And teach your kids!

- If you travel frequently, keep a toilet article bag prepacked and ready to go.

- Not enough can be said about coming into the office 30 minutes early or staying 30 minutes late for uninterrupted planning, reading and just plain work time.

- At home, turn off the TV for 30 minutes to catch up on phone calls and tasks that have gone undone. What does 30 minutes give you? An additional 183 hours per year. Is watching that rerun again really that important?

- Reward yourself during an unpleasant task. Play upbeat music, have a special cup of coffee or tea. Decide how you will further reward yourself when the task is complete. Give yourself the incentive to get the job done.

- Place motivational or inspirational quotes around your workspace or on your computer's screen saver to help you overcome your most difficult issues and remain upbeat.

Add one new organizational tip per week to your routine. Make a note on your calendar and to-do lists and little by little, you will be the envy of all of the packrats and organizationally impaired people around you.

INDEX

Buy any 3, get 1 FREE!

Get a 60-Minute Training Series™ Handbook FREE ($14.95 value)* when you buy any three. See back of order form for full selection of titles.

These are helpful how-to books for you, your employees and co-workers. Add to your library. Use for new-employee training, brown-bag seminars, promotion gifts and more. Choose from many popular titles on a variety of lifestyle, communication, productivity and leadership topics. Exclusively from National Press Publications.

DESKTOP HANDBOOK ORDER FORM

Ordering is easy:

1. Complete both sides of this Order Form, detach, and mail, fax or phone your order to:

   Mail: National Press Publications
   P.O. Box 419107
   Kansas City, MO 64141-6107

   Fax: 1-913-432-0824

   Phone: 1-800-258-7248 (in Canada 1-800-685-4142)

2. Please print:

Name _____ Position/Title _____

Company/Organization _____

Address _____ City _____

State/Province _____ ZIP/Postal Code _____

Telephone(____) _____ Fax (____) _____

3. Easy payment:

❑ Enclosed is my check or money order for $_____ (total from back).
Please make payable to National Press Publications.

Please charge to:
❑ MasterCard   ❑ VISA   ❑ American Express

Credit Card No._____ Exp. Date _____

Signature _____

• •
MORE WAYS TO SAVE:

SAVE 33%!!! BUY 20-50 COPIES of any title ... pay just $9.95 each ($11.25 Canadian).
SAVE 40%!!! BUY 51 COPIES OR MORE of any title ... pay just $8.95 each ($10.25 Canadian).
*$16.95 in Canada

Buy 3, get 1 FREE!
60-MINUTE TRAINING SERIES™ HANDBOOKS

TITLE	RETAIL PRICE	QTY.	TOTAL
8 Steps for Highly Effective Negotiations #424	$14.95		
Assertiveness #442	$14.95		
Balancing Career and Family #415	$14.95		
Change: Coping with Tomorrow Today #421	$14.95		
Customer Service: The Key ... Customers #488	$14.95		
Empowering the Self-Directed Team #422	$14.95		
Fear &-Anger: Slay the Dragons ... #4302	$14.95		
Getting Things Done #4112	$14.95		
How to Conduct Win-Win Perf. Appraisals #423	$14.95		
How to De-Junk Your Life #4306	$14.95		
How to Manage Conflict #495	$14.95		
How to Manage Your Boss #493	$14.95		
How to Supervise People #4102	$14.95		
Listen Up: Hear What's Really Being Said #4172	$14.95		
Diversity — Managing Our Differences #412	$14.95		
Motivation and Goal-Setting #4962	$14.95		
A New Attitude #4432	$14.95		
PC Survival Guide #407	$14.95		
Parenting: Ward & June ... #486	$14.95		
Peak Performance #469	$14.95		
Powerful Communication Skills #4132	$14.95		
The Polished Professional #426	$14.95		
The Power of Innovative Thinking #428	$14.95		
Powerful Leadership Skills for Women #463	$14.95		
Powerful Presentation Skills #461	$14.95		
Self-Esteem: The Power to Be Your Best #4642	$14.95		
SELF Profile #403	$14.95		
The Stress Management Handbook #4842	$14.95		
Supreme Teams: How to Make Teams Work #4303	$14.95		
Techniques to Improve Your Writing Skills #460	$14.95		
The Windows Handbook #4304	$14.95		

Sales Tax		
All purchases subject to state and local sales tax. Questions? Call 1-800-258-7248	Subtotal	$
	Add 7% Sales Tax *(Or add appropriate state and local tax)*	$
	Shipping and Handling *($3 one item; 50¢ each additional item)*	$

Buy any 3, get 1 FREE!

Get a 60-Minute Training Series™ Handbook FREE ($14.95 value)*
when you buy any three. See back of order form for full selection of titles.

These are helpful how-to books for you, your employees and co-workers. Add to your library. Use for new-employee training, brown-bag seminars, promotion gifts and more. Choose from many popular titles on a variety of lifestyle, communication, productivity and leadership topics. Exclusively from National Press Publications.

DESKTOP HANDBOOK ORDER FORM

Ordering is easy:

1. Complete both sides of this Order Form, detach, and mail, fax or phone your order to:
   Mail: National Press Publications
   P.O. Box 419107
   Kansas City, MO 64141-6107
   Fax: 1-913-432-0824
   Phone: 1-800-258-7248 (in Canada 1-800-685-4142)

2. Please print:

Name _____ Position/Title _____

Company/Organization _____

Address _____ City _____

State/Province _____ ZIP/Postal Code _____

Telephone(____) _____ Fax (____) _____

3. Easy payment:

❑ Enclosed is my check or money order for $_____ (total from back).
Please make payable to National Press Publications.

Please charge to:
❑ MasterCard   ❑ VISA   ❑ American Express

Credit Card No._____ Exp. Date _____

Signature _____

● ●

MORE WAYS TO SAVE:

SAVE 33%!!! BUY 20-50 COPIES of any title ... pay just $9.95 each ($11.25 Canadian).
SAVE 40%!!! BUY 51 COPIES OR MORE of any title ... pay just $8.95 each ($10.25 Canadian).
*$16.95 in Canada

Buy 3, get 1 FREE!
60-MINUTE TRAINING SERIES™ HANDBOOKS

TITLE	RETAIL PRICE	QTY.	TOTAL
8 Steps for Highly Effective Negotiations #424	$14.95		
Assertiveness #442	$14.95		
Balancing Career and Family #415	$14.95		
Change: Coping with Tomorrow Today #421	$14.95		
Customer Service: The Key ... Customers #488	$14.95		
Empowering the Self-Directed Team #422	$14.95		
Fear &-Anger: Slay the Dragons ... #4302	$14.95		
Getting Things Done #4112	$14.95		
How to Conduct Win-Win Perf. Appraisals #423	$14.95		
How to De-Junk Your Life #4306	$14.95		
How to Manage Conflict #495	$14.95		
How to Manage Your Boss #493	$14.95		
How to Supervise People #4102	$14.95		
Listen Up: Hear What's Really Being Said #4172	$14.95		
Diversity — Managing Our Differences #412	$14.95		
Motivation and Goal-Setting #4962	$14.95		
A New Attitude #4432	$14.95		
PC Survival Guide #407	$14.95		
Parenting: Ward & June ... #486	$14.95		
Peak Performance #469	$14.95		
Powerful Communication Skills #4132	$14.95		
The Polished Professional #426	$14.95		
The Power of Innovative Thinking #428	$14.95		
Powerful Leadership Skills for Women #463	$14.95		
Powerful Presentation Skills #461	$14.95		
Self-Esteem: The Power to Be Your Best #4642	$14.95		
SELF Profile #403	$14.95		
The Stress Management Handbook #4842	$14.95		
Supreme Teams: How to Make Teams Work #4303	$14.95		
Techniques to Improve Your Writing Skills #460	$14.95		
The Windows Handbook #4304	$14.95		

Sales Tax All purchases subject to state and local sales tax. Questions? Call **1-800-258-7248**	**Subtotal**	$
	Add 7% Sales Tax *(Or add appropriate state and local tax)*	$
	Shipping and Handling *($3 one item; 50¢ each additional item)*	$

Buy any 3, get 1 FREE!

Get a 60-Minute Training Series™ Handbook FREE ($14.95 value)*
when you buy any three. See back of order form for full selection of titles.

These are helpful how-to books for you, your employees and co-workers. Add to your library. Use for new-employee training, brown-bag seminars, promotion gifts and more. Choose from many popular titles on a variety of lifestyle, communication, productivity and leadership topics. Exclusively from National Press Publications.

DESKTOP HANDBOOK ORDER FORM

Ordering is easy:

1. Complete both sides of this Order Form, detach, and mail, fax or phone your order to:
   Mail: National Press Publications
   P.O. Box 419107
   Kansas City, MO 64141-6107
   Fax: 1-913-432-0824
   Phone: 1-800-258-7248 (in Canada 1-800-685-4142)

2. Please print:

Name _____ Position/Title _____

Company/Organization _____

Address _____ City _____

State/Province _____ ZIP/Postal Code _____

Telephone(____) _____ Fax (____) _____

3. Easy payment:

❑ Enclosed is my check or money order for $_____ (total from back).
Please make payable to National Press Publications.

Please charge to:
❑ MasterCard   ❑ VISA   ❑ American Express

Credit Card No._____ Exp. Date _____

Signature _____

●●●●●●●●●●●●●●●●●●●●●●●●●●●●●●●●●●●●●●

MORE WAYS TO SAVE:

SAVE 33%!!! BUY 20-50 COPIES of any title ... pay just $9.95 each ($11.25 Canadian).
SAVE 40%!!! BUY 51 COPIES OR MORE of any title ... pay just $8.95 each ($10.25 Canadian).
*$16.95 in Canada

Buy 3, get 1 FREE!
60-MINUTE TRAINING SERIES™ HANDBOOKS

TITLE	RETAIL PRICE	QTY.	TOTAL
8 Steps for Highly Effective Negotiations #424	$14.95		
Assertiveness #442	$14.95		
Balancing Career and Family #415	$14.95		
Change: Coping with Tomorrow Today #421	$14.95		
Customer Service: The Key ... Customers #488	$14.95		
Empowering the Self-Directed Team #422	$14.95		
Fear &-Anger: Slay the Dragons ... #4302	$14.95		
Getting Things Done #4112	$14.95		
How to Conduct Win-Win Perf. Appraisals #423	$14.95		
How to De-Junk Your Life #4306	$14.95		
How to Manage Conflict #495	$14.95		
How to Manage Your Boss #493	$14.95		
How to Supervise People #4102	$14.95		
Listen Up: Hear What's Really Being Said #4172	$14.95		
Diversity — Managing Our Differences #412	$14.95		
Motivation and Goal-Setting #4962	$14.95		
A New Attitude #4432	$14.95		
PC Survival Guide #407	$14.95		
Parenting: Ward & June ... #486	$14.95		
Peak Performance #469	$14.95		
Powerful Communication Skills #4132	$14.95		
The Polished Professional #426	$14.95		
The Power of Innovative Thinking #428	$14.95		
Powerful Leadership Skills for Women #463	$14.95		
Powerful Presentation Skills #461	$14.95		
Self-Esteem: The Power to Be Your Best #4642	$14.95		
SELF Profile #403	$14.95		
The Stress Management Handbook #4842	$14.95		
Supreme Teams: How to Make Teams Work #4303	$14.95		
Techniques to Improve Your Writing Skills #460	$14.95		
The Windows Handbook #4304	$14.95		

Sales Tax	Subtotal	$
All purchases subject to state and local sales tax. Questions? Call **1-800-258-7248**	**Add 7% Sales Tax** *(Or add appropriate state and local tax)*	$
	Shipping and Handling *($3 one item; 50¢ each additional item)*	$

Buy any 3, get 1 FREE!

Get a 60-Minute Training Series™ Handbook FREE ($14.95 value)* when you buy any three. See back of order form for full selection of titles.

These are helpful how-to books for you, your employees and co-workers. Add to your library. Use for new-employee training, brown-bag seminars, promotion gifts and more. Choose from many popular titles on a variety of lifestyle, communication, productivity and leadership topics. Exclusively from National Press Publications.

DESKTOP HANDBOOK ORDER FORM

Ordering is easy:

1. Complete both sides of this Order Form, detach, and mail, fax or phone your order to:

      Mail: National Press Publications
      P.O. Box 419107
      Kansas City, MO 64141-6107

  Fax: 1-913-432-0824

  Phone: 1-800-258-7248 (in Canada 1-800-685-4142)

2. Please print:

Name _____ Position/Title _____

Company/Organization _____

Address _____ City _____

State/Province _____ ZIP/Postal Code _____

Telephone(___) _____ Fax (___) _____

3. Easy payment:

❑ Enclosed is my check or money order for $_____ (total from back).
Please make payable to National Press Publications.

Please charge to:
❑ MasterCard   ❑ VISA   ❑ American Express

Credit Card No. _____ Exp. Date _____

Signature _____

• •

MORE WAYS TO SAVE:

SAVE 33%!!! BUY 20-50 COPIES of any title ... pay just $9.95 each ($11.25 Canadian).
SAVE 40%!!! BUY 51 COPIES OR MORE of any title ... pay just $8.95 each ($10.25 Canadian).
*$16.95 in Canada

Buy 3, get 1 FREE!
60-MINUTE TRAINING SERIES™ HANDBOOKS

TITLE	RETAIL PRICE	QTY.	TOTAL
8 Steps for Highly Effective Negotiations #424	$14.95		
Assertiveness #442	$14.95		
Balancing Career and Family #415	$14.95		
Change: Coping with Tomorrow Today #421	$14.95		
Customer Service: The Key ... Customers #488	$14.95		
Empowering the Self-Directed Team #422	$14.95		
Fear &-Anger: Slay the Dragons ... #4302	$14.95		
Getting Things Done #4112	$14.95		
How to Conduct Win-Win Perf. Appraisals #423	$14.95		
How to De-Junk Your Life #4306	$14.95		
How to Manage Conflict #495	$14.95		
How to Manage Your Boss #493	$14.95		
How to Supervise People #4102	$14.95		
Listen Up: Hear What's Really Being Said #4172	$14.95		
Diversity — Managing Our Differences #412	$14.95		
Motivation and Goal-Setting #4962	$14.95		
A New Attitude #4432	$14.95		
PC Survival Guide #407	$14.95		
Parenting: Ward & June ... #486	$14.95		
Peak Performance #469	$14.95		
Powerful Communication Skills #4132	$14.95		
The Polished Professional #426	$14.95		
The Power of Innovative Thinking #428	$14.95		
Powerful Leadership Skills for Women #463	$14.95		
Powerful Presentation Skills #461	$14.95		
Self-Esteem: The Power to Be Your Best #4642	$14.95		
SELF Profile #403	$14.95		
The Stress Management Handbook #4842	$14.95		
Supreme Teams: How to Make Teams Work #4303	$14.95		
Techniques to Improve Your Writing Skills #460	$14.95		
The Windows Handbook #4304	$14.95		

Sales Tax		
Sales Tax All purchases subject to state and local sales tax. Questions? Call **1-800-258-7248**	**Subtotal**	$
	Add 7% Sales Tax *(Or add appropriate state and local tax)*	$
	Shipping and Handling *($3 one item; 50¢ each additional item)*	$